All rights reserved. No part of this publication can be reproduced, stored in a retrieval system, or transmitted in any in form or by any means, mechanical, photocopying, recording or otherwise, without the prior expressed written permission, from the publisher, Capstone Media Services or the author. Copyright of most of the images is the property of the author, other images used have granted copyright consent. While every effort has been made to contact copyright holders for consent to use some images, in some instances copyright holders have been untraceable for which we offer or sincere apologise. Such images have therefore been acknowledged in the source notation and photographic credits at the back of this book.

Memorabilia

This book contains events and experiences worthy of remembrance and contains memorabilia that tells the life of the legendary Dame Elizabeth Taylor.

Dame Elizabeth Taylor
shades of violet

A story told in memorabilia by
Wayne Griffin

Contents

Memorabilia...iv

Foreword 1

Dedication 3

One fan's personal tribute.. 4

Wildwood Road Hampstead 5

The personal photograph 8

The vintage family photograph....................................... 11

The White Cliffs of Dover 15

National Velvet screen worn wig..................................... 16

The vintage clutch 31

The Helena Rubinstein lip stick 32

The mechanical pencil 34

The vintage beaded necklace... 35

Elizabeth's written hand 37

The rose hair clip 38

The hairclip dish.. 39

The Wedding gift 46

The MGM hand coloured portrait 50

The bow head dress 51

The silk head dress 52

The gold hair bush 57

The hair brush set.. 58

The hair curlers 59

The cotton white gloves 60

The antique rhinestone necklace.....................................61

The many brooches	62
The Elizabeth Taylor fan club	70
The Last Time I saw Paris screen worn wig	74
Raintree County screen worn crinoline	84
The Raintree County Picnic	87
The watch pendant	89
The embellished silver bracelet	91
The Raintree dinner party	92
Elizabeth in Australia	99
Double Breasted Herringbone Coat	101
The green crystal pin brooch	103
The clear crystal perfume bottle	108
The wedding gown	110
Crystal Jewelry Dish	111
The set of vases	112
The black lycra elbow length gloves	115
The faux poodle jacket / cape	119
The Vintage Brooch	121
The faux Ruby and Diamond earrings	125
The faux Ruby and Diamond pendant necklace	126
The Cleopatra costume	128
The Victorian rocking chair	130
The Cleopatra movie props	132
The lost paparazzi shots	136
Elizabeth poolside, 1963	138
The crepe hat	139
The cream woolen pants	140
Mrs. Richard Burton	141

The personal copy of National Velvet	144
The Italian head wrap	147
Mrs. Burton's private jet	149
The jewelry case	154
The powder blue coat	157
The drinking glass	159
The sterling silver money clip	160
The maxi dress	164
The red woolen pants	165
The Jaguar fur coat	166
The costume brooch	167
The director's chair	168
The bathing suit	170
The lace skirt	171
The plaid woolen pants	172
The Casa Kimberly estate collection	175
The ashtray	175
Collection of head scarves	176
The maxi dress	177
The paper mache figurines	178
The glass ice bucket	179
The persimmon background	180
The cotton shirt dress	181
The blouse and trouser ensemble	182
The embroidered blouse	183
The lavender crystal perfume bottle	184
The alumesh handbag	185
Head scarf	188

The Valentino pant suit	189
The Valentino green turtle neck	191
The chiffon evening gown	195
The bufferfly and circle dress	197
The pillbox	201
Elizabeth declines a party invitation	203
The vintage faux ruby bracelet	204
The waist length jacket	207
The black leather bootss	210
The Laura Biagiotti sunglasses	214
Elizabeth's letter of condolence	216
The cashmere blanket	217
The North and South velvet gown	223
The evening dress	226
The Oscar Gown	227
The sequined evening gown	228
The Poker Alice screen worn shoes	233
The pink satin costume	234
The deep garnet moiré taffeta costume	236
The Poker Alice faux playing cards	238
Poker Alice screen worn gown	239
The periwinkle blue wool hat	240
Dearest Elizabeth.....the first correspondence	241
The satin pyjamas	246
The rhinestone brooch	247
The American Hope Awards promotional jacket	252
The birthday napkin	260
The gift from Italy	263

The White Diamond perfume bottle	265
The chiffon wrap	269
The lavender satin and rhinestone clutch	281
The open-toed shoes	282
The violet and pink belts	283
The birthday card	285
The two-piece suit	286
The signed script	293
Pure intensity and brilliance	301
The white silk handkerchief	304
The denim hat	305
The lavender manuscript	308
The final letter	310
The final shade of violet	312
Dame Elizabeth rest in peace	318
The largest memorabilia auction in history	319
My homage to Dame Elizabeth Taylor	321
Dame Elizabeth's favourite cocktail	323
Dame Elizabeth Taylor- shades of violet	323
The Queen of Celebrity Activism	325
Photographic credits	333
Special resources	334

Foreword

Once upon a time the word 'star' applied to someone fabulous who worked in the entertainment business. It was an accolade for those with a magnetism, glamour, and quality that set them apart from mere mortals. Then came the era of celebrity when the industry was created around people who were famous for actually being famous. Fodder for the phony celebrity mill that made headlines for all the wrong reasons, none of them having anything to do with talent. So how do we describe a star that was a star and not just a headline? They became a 'superstar' and when that word was devalued, we made them a "megastar".

Desperate girls draped over products in game shows, people forecasting the weather on news programs and talking heads on panel shows are sometimes a diversion but are not stars, superstars, megastars or magnum stars. Modern day films are often cast with people who would not turn your head on an escalator, people with the personality of burnt toast and actors who have less radiance than a flashlight. Elizabeth… just say her name and you'll think star in all its scintillating incandescence.

Elizabeth – never 'Liz' –always Elizabeth was not just one of the world's most beautiful and alluring women but an accomplished actress, who was willing to shed the image of perfect beauty when the role required it of her. In an era when children of the rich and famous are often poster material for being troubled or in trouble, Elizabeth's family are a true testament to her role as a mother, even as her personal life made news around the world.

Stars, who are real stars, are a person who is under the spotlight and that's how I would describe Dame Elizabeth. When Elizabeth enters a room, you see a radiance that beguiles everyone. If you are fortunate enough to be close enough to look into those violet eyes you can understand how so many men wilted and fell in love with her.

When you hear Elizabeth's soft voice it's as if you are in a close up with her in, Giant, The VIPs, Cleopatra, Cat on a Hot Tin Roof and a score of other movies that have made her a living legend. Elizabeth has captivated several generations and when we look at her films, sometimes less interesting than her real life saga, we see what the word, star, really means. Elizabeth was, is, and will always be a star in every sense of the word.

'I first met the late Elizabeth in 1993 at the LA Equestrian Centre when she was launching, '*White Diamonds*.' 'Dearest Elizabeth was extraordinarily beautiful and gracious.'

By Sir John Michael Howson

John Michael Howson, OAM - Australian Author, Writer, and Media Commentator.

Source: Sir John Michael Howson.

Dedication

These works are dedicated to my partner Chris, who at many times during the thousands of hours spent researching and collating this book, often mentioned that he thought that I was, in fact, more in love with Elizabeth than with him. To all my friends and family who have watched this private collection grow and have listened to my trials and tribulations and to the angels who have guided me through this enormous process especially my late grandparents Heather and Ron Newhill and all the other loved ones I have lost along the way.

I can't forget the hours spent with Peter Francis, my confidant, my agent and my inspiration in turning my dream into reality. Peter and the Capstone team were wonderful in the Dame Elizabeth shades of violet experience and were the guiding light when darkness fell, and Mr. P's inspiration and desire to achieve the best has prevailed and been a master component of this project. I must also thank Capstone Media Services for providing me with an exceptional opportunity to bring my story, my book and my private collection to the world.

Finally to the lady whom without a doubt is the perfect essence of true celebrity, Dame Elizabeth, thank you for adding endless hours of joy, excitement, and passion to our world and without whom, this private collection could never have been made possible.

One fan's personal tribute

Dame Elizabeth grew from a doll-faced child starlet to become one of the silver screen's most celebrated and striking beauties. From her first public appearance to her affairs of the nineteen sixties, her passion for expensive jewels, and her endless commitment for human equality, Elizabeth was a natural magnet for publicity throughout her 70-year movie star career.

Holding the record for being the most photographed woman in history, including her 14 appearances on the cover of Life Magazine. Sometimes her notoriety overshadowed her accomplishments. Elizabeth received five Best Actress nominations, three Academy Awards, a BAFTA award along with many other accolades over her seven-decade career.

Never will you see such a compelling and fascinating collection showcased in all its beauty, including personal items from Elizabeth's very own wardrobe, personal letters from her and other stars, along with some of the most breathtaking images ever to be seen. Never released paparazzi photographs of Elizabeth's private affairs disclose an endless beauty far more alluring than any of her performances on the big screen.

Dame Elizabeth Taylor shades of violet- a story told in memorabilia tells not only the story of an extraordinary life of the last queen of Hollywood, it is also tells a remarkable story of celebrity connection made possible through the many items in this collection.

Many people have asked if I have ever met this Hollywood icon and I often reply, 'I meet Elizabeth every time I see items from this private collection' and so will you.

Wildwood Road Hampstead

Francis Lenn Taylor and Sara Viola Southern were married in 1926 and gave birth to their first child, Howard Taylor in 1929. His sister was born at 2.15am on February 27, 1932, in a small cottage at the end of Wildwood Road, North London. Elizabeth Rosemond Taylor was born with exceptional looks, but also doubled rowed eyelashes and those most famous violet eyes.

Sara Taylor holds her two month old daughter, Elizabeth Rosemond Taylor, 1932.

Sara Taylor with her 2 ½-year-old daughter *Elizabeth*, and her son *Howard*.

 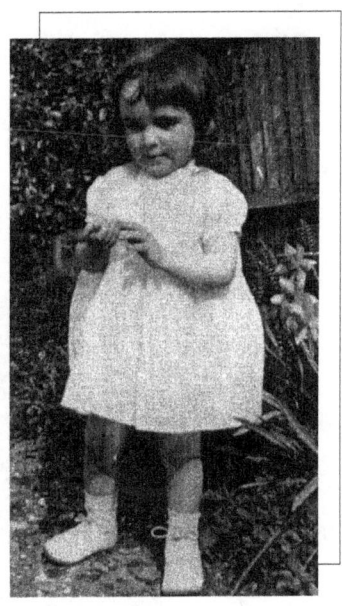

Elizabeth at three years of age plays in her garden at the Taylor's Wildwood road cottage in England, 1935.

Source: Gladys Culverhouse (the Taylor's maid at the time).

My brother Howard was 5½ and I was only 3½ when dad took this picture

The personal photograph

This photograph was originally the property of Elizabeth Taylor. She has inscribed details about the photograph on the back and in doing so gifted it to Ruth Culverhouse, who was a friend to Elizabeth Taylor when her mother Glenys and father George worked in the Taylor home. After Ruth passed away many years later, her son, Bryan Hamilton sold the item to the collection. A portrait of Elizabeth and her brother Howard taken by their father Francis in 1935.

At the age of three, Elizabeth made her very first public appearance, dressed as a beautiful butterfly, she mesmerised the adoring public, in Madam Vercconi's 1935 concert for the Royal Family. Transfixed, Elizabeth bowed and bowed and it seemed the more the public applauded her the more she would bow until she was the last to leave the stage. The public became hypnotised by Elizabeth's beauty for the first time and would remain transfixed and fascinated by her beauty for the rest of her living days and beyond.

With World War II on the horizon, Sara Taylor and her family left England in June 1939 and relocated to the Californian hills, where Frances was to join his family later and establish himself as a leading art dealer at the Beverly Hills Hotel. Utilising various contacts made through Francis Taylor's business, Elizabeth met Universal's producer John Constantine on September 18, 1941 and was signed to a six-month renewable contract at $100 per week. Elizabeth's first on-screen appearance was in the Universal motion picture, *There's One Born Every Minute*, with stars Catherine Doucette and little Alfalfa Sweetzer.

Edward Muhl, the studio's production chief declared 'Elizabeth can't dance, sing and her eyes look too old for a child' and consequently, *There's One Born Every Minute* would be Elizabeth's first and only film for Universal Pictures and eight months later her contract was terminated. She was then signed to Metro Goldwyn Mayer for $100 a week, to appear as Priscilla in the Fred M Wilcox, 1943 film, *Lassie Come Home*.

Elizabeth remained with MGM for the next 18 years.

The vintage family photograph

This photograph of Dame Elizabeth Taylor, her brother Howard and mother Sara was taken by Gladys Culverhouse (staff) outside their Hampstead home, North London, England, en route to the USA.

Mr. and Mrs. Culverhouse who worked for the Taylor's would soon join them in the US sometime later. The image was first the property of the Taylor's housekeeper, Glenys Culverhouse who gifted it to her daughter Ruth who was a friend to Elizabeth Taylor. Ruth kept the photograph for many years in a safe place and when she passed away, her son Bryan Hamilton sold it to this collection.

Ruth's parents, George and Gladys Culverhouse became personal assistants to the Taylor household. Gladys was employed as the housekeeper and George the maintenance guy and chauffeur. It was George Culverhouse that taught Elizabeth to take her first steps, and no one knew they would lead Elizabeth to such celebrity and stardom.

Elizabeth, her brother Howard and her mother Sara left their home on June 19, 1939 to take their voyage across the sea to the US. They are pictured here in the last image of them together at 8 Wildwood Rd, Hampstead, North London.

It would be several years later before the Taylor's would send for their staff to join them in their new found homeland.

Source: Glenys Culverhouse, Bryan Hamilton and Sara Taylor.

Pictured here are some rare and exclusive photographs of Elizabeth's childhood friend, Ruth Culverhouse. She is pictured here playing in the Taylor's front garden of their Hampstead Estate, 1939.

Source: Glenys and George Culverhouse, Ruth Culverhouse and Bryan Hamilton.

Elizabeth is pictured here in her very first movie role in the film, *There's one born every minute*.

In the following year Elizabeth appeared in two minor films *The White Cliffs of Dover* opposite Roddy McDowall and Robert Stevenson's film *Jane Eyre* before securing the part of Velvet Brown in the 1945 MGM classic movie *National Velvet*.

National Velvet hit the silver screens on October 4, 1945 and turned Elizabeth into an overnight movie star sensation. At twelve, Elizabeth, a star, was now earning a salary of $30,000 a year. The film grossed over 4.4 million dollars and left Elizabeth a legacy of back pain, after a fall from the horse during filming crushed two of her lower vertebrae. The studio gave her the horse (King Charles) and she would have him until his death. As a consequence, Elizabeth would remain wheelchair-bound in her later years.

Elizabeth Taylor is pictured meeting Roddy McDowell at her front gate wearing the chequered costume.

The White Cliffs of Dover

This chequered pinafore was worn on set by Elizabeth Taylor in the 1944 film, *The White Cliffs of Dover* and is deemed to be one of the oldest items in the collection. This is a child size blue and white chequered pinafore with single lace trim. It has two front pockets and a bib style top with butterfly styles shoulders. The costume ties nicely at the back.

Elizabeth Taylor was 12 years old at the time and co-starred with Roddy McDowell, who later became one of her lifelong friends, starring with her again in *Lassie Come Home* and in a later film, *Cleopatra*. This costume was stored in the costume department at MGM studios before Heritage Auctions obtained it.

Source: Butterfield and Butterfield auctions USA.

National Velvet screen worn wig

This beautiful brown wig was worn by Elizabeth Taylor for her break-out role as Velvet Brown in the 1944 multiple Oscar-winning family classic *National Velvet*. It is hand-tied and made from human hair and includes the original Max Factor box and the MGM wig stock record card. The wig originated from MGM Wig Works.

Source: Manufacture by Wig Works Studios California/ MGM Studios.

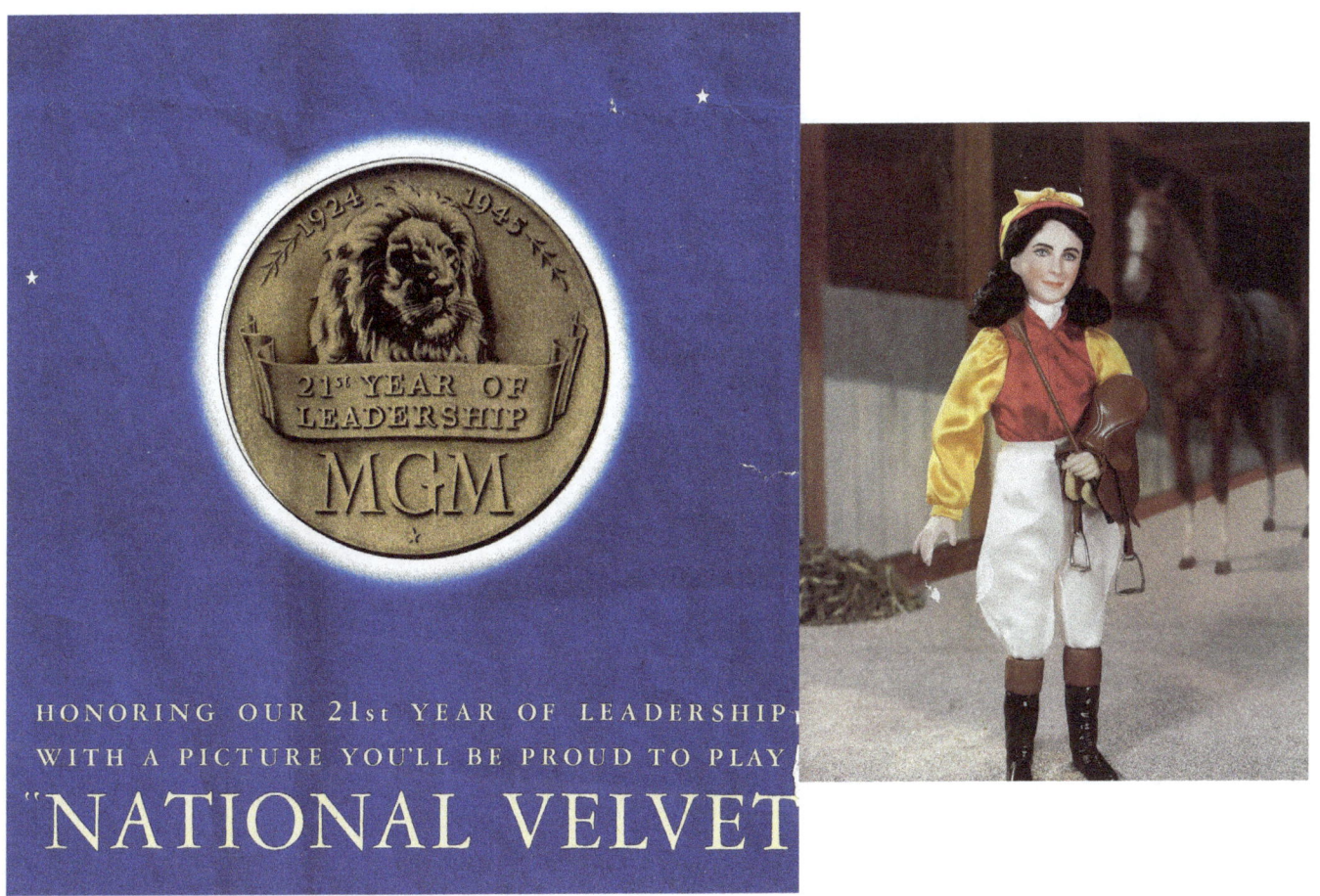

In 1945, MGM released the *National Velvet* hat to coincide with the release of the film.

MGM also released the *National Velvet* celebrity doll to coincide with the release of the film. The likeness is so carefully hand painted to capture Elizabeth's captivating violet eyes, 1945.

Source: Franklin Heirloom Dolls/MGM.

Elizabeth was now a star and this is one of the very original stars autographs.

Source: National Velvet program, 1945.

'Elizabeth as Velvet Brown, Flawless and enchanting portrayal... a materialized dream of wholesome loveliness.' – The New York Time

In 1946, Elizabeth wrote the very first of her four biographies this one was more about her love affair with her beautiful nine pet chipmunks and was titled, *Nibbles and Me*. However, all the beauty in the world could not prevent the sad demise of the Taylor family and in November 1946, Sara and Francis Taylor separated after 20 years of marriage.

Gossip columnist at the time Hedda Hopper proclaimed Elizabeth to be 'the most beautiful woman in America.'

Elizabeth's first of four biographies, this one was more about her nine pet chipmunks than herself, 1946.

Source: Duell, Sloan & Pearce.

'Working with horses and dogs was no great work; it was like playing myself for two months and the studio even gave me the horse.'

- Elizabeth Taylor

Capitalising on the huge box office success of *National Velvet*, Elizabeth was cast in another animal film, this time her co-star was Bill the canine, in another Fred M Wilcox production, *Courage of Lassie*. Elizabeth had now gained a reputation as a bankable adolescent actor promising her a full career with MGM and in 1947 she was loaned to Warner Bros for her next two films, *Life with Father* and the Robert Z Leonard directed film, *Cynthia*.

'Elizabeth Taylor took off just like a lovely bird.' -Angela Lansbury

Pictured here is Elizabeth Taylor with her co-star Bill in a scene from *Courage of Lassie*.

Safely returned from the blizzard, with the lamb she had risked her life to rescue!

MGM presents LASSIE in COURAGE of LASSIE in Technicolor
ELIZABETH TAYLOR · FRANK MORGAN · TOM DR...

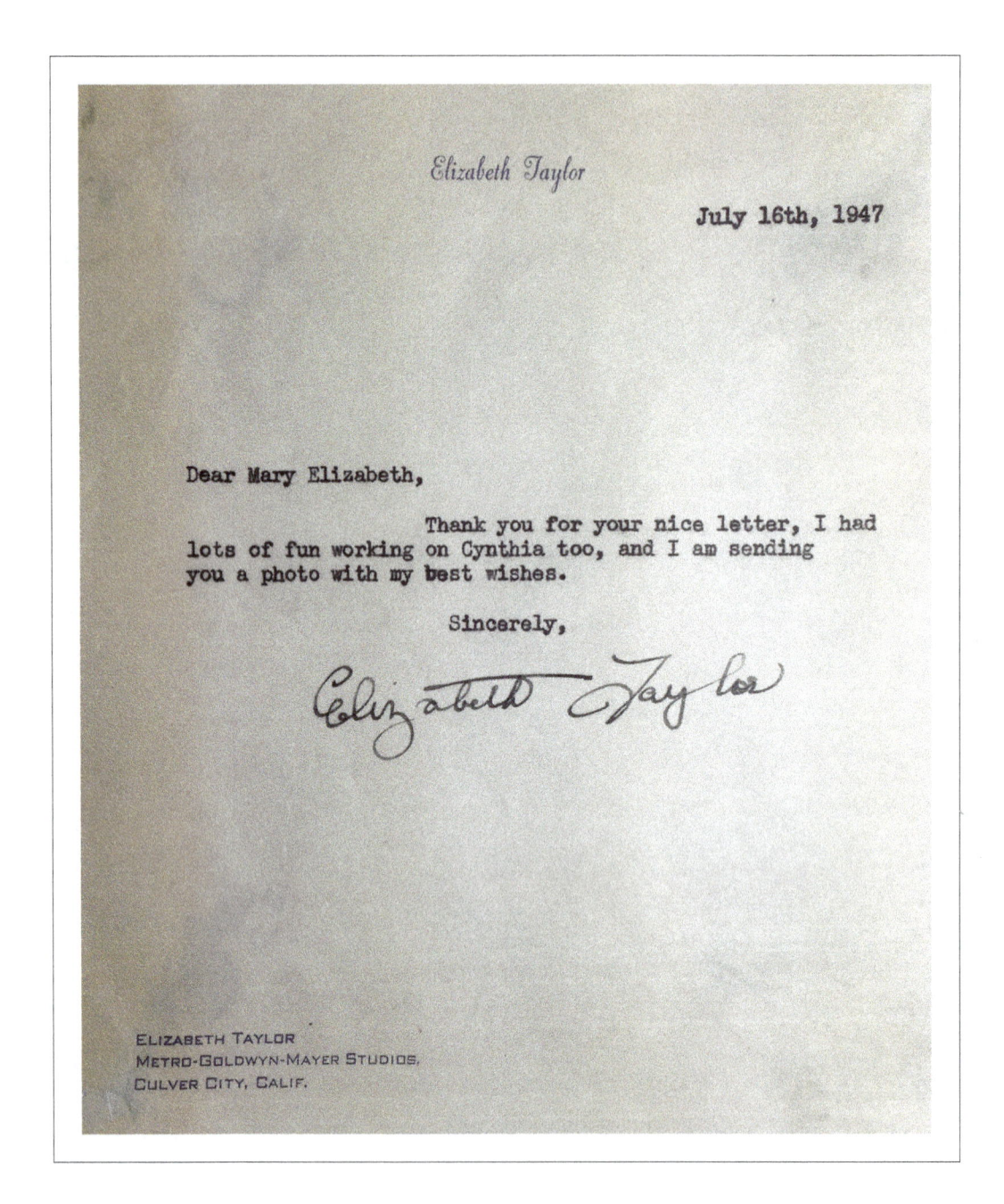

In this original letter, Elizabeth talks about her work on the MGM film *Cynthia*, 1947.

Source: George Houle books and autographs, Los Angeles.

In this original handwritten letter, Elizabeth talks about King Charles, the horse MGM gave her after filming *National Velvet* and her work on her new film, *Little Women*.

Elizabeth soon earned the title of 'One shot Liz', as she was able to shoot most scenes in one take and was now earning $2000 a week. The last of her adolesent films would include *A Date with Judy* 1948, *Julia Misbehaves* and the 1949 American classic, *Little Women*. While the adoring public may not have been ready to be seduced by Elizabeth's newfound sexuality, the movie-making machines of the nineteen fifties were.

In 1949, Sara Taylor joined her daughter in England for Elizabeth's first adult role opposite Robert Taylor in the film *The Conspirator*. It was during the filming of this film that Elizabeth first met Michael Wilding (39) and later went onto date millionaire Howard Hughes, breaking off the relationship to later marry 23-year-old, hotel heir, Nicolas Hilton.

Elizabeth now 17 experienced her very first fan extortion and made the front page of the Los Angeles Examiner on November 20, 1949. Her personal life would remain public interest for the rest of her living days.

Elizabeth appears on the front page of a local morning newspaper.

Source: Los Angeles Examiner.

Elizabeth Taylor Guarded at Studio After Extort Try

TARGET OF NOTES—Three threatening extortion letters from New York have been received by Actress Elizabeth Taylor (above), it was revealed yesterday. She is closely guarded.
—Nat Dallinger photo, copyright, King Features Syndicate, Inc.

Money Demand Made on Film Star in Letters From N.Y.

Three extortion notes threatening harm to Elizabeth Taylor of the screen were under investigation yesterday.

Miss Taylor, who, at 17, has been called Hollywood's most beautiful girl, is under guard.

Special precautions were taken at Paramount Studio, where she s on loan from Metro-Goldwyn-

It was understood Miss Taylor, as they arrived, consulted Whitey Hendry, studio chief of police at M-G-M.

30

The vintage clutch

This patch worked clutch is made up of small squares of animal hide. Elizabeth is pictured wearing the clutch as she and her mother stroll down the main street in London. Ruth's mum, Gladys and her father, George began their employment as part of the Taylor's service staff in 1929. Ruth and Elizabeth became childhood friends as a result.

Ruth Culverhouse wrote a book on her experience with the Taylor's. An image from her book "So Blessed" shows Ruth Culverhouse with the clutch purse given to her by Elizabeth Taylor when they were childhood friends. After Elizabeth Taylor gifted the clutch to Ruth Culverhouse, the clutch had been stored in her personal belongings for over 60 years. Ruth's eldest son, Bryan Hamilton sold it to the collection after his mother passed in 2010.

The Helena Rubinstein lip stick

This miniature Helena Rubinstein lipstick is enclosed in a gold rippled casing. It was found inside the animal patch bag Elizabeth Taylor used during a trip to England with her mother Sara in 1949. It is believed that she used it to touch up her makeup on and off the movie set. The lipstick measures 2 1/4 inches tall x 5/8 inch diameter with a twist mechanism that works.

Source: Ruth Culverhouse estate, Bryan Hamilton son of Ruth Culverhouse and Helena Rubinstein.

'There are no ugly women, only lazy ones'
– Helena Rubinstein

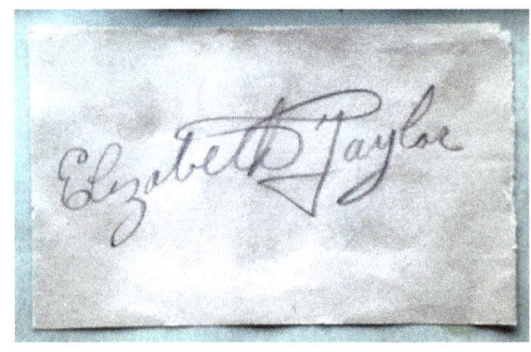

The mechanical pencil

Now that Elizabeth had become a household name, she would be stopped in the street by autograph-seeking fans. Some of Elizabeth's very first hand signed autographs were done in mechanical pencil. This is one of the pencils Elizabeth used to carry with her when meeting fans of her work.

Source: Ron, personal assistant to Elizabeth from 1947-1971/Lisa Jones.

The vintage beaded necklace

This is a double-stranded faux white pearl necklace with 24 carat gold accents. The beads are oblong in shape. The necklace measures 14 inches in diameter. An item originally gifted from Elizabeth Taylor to a make-up artist to the stars Ben Nye.

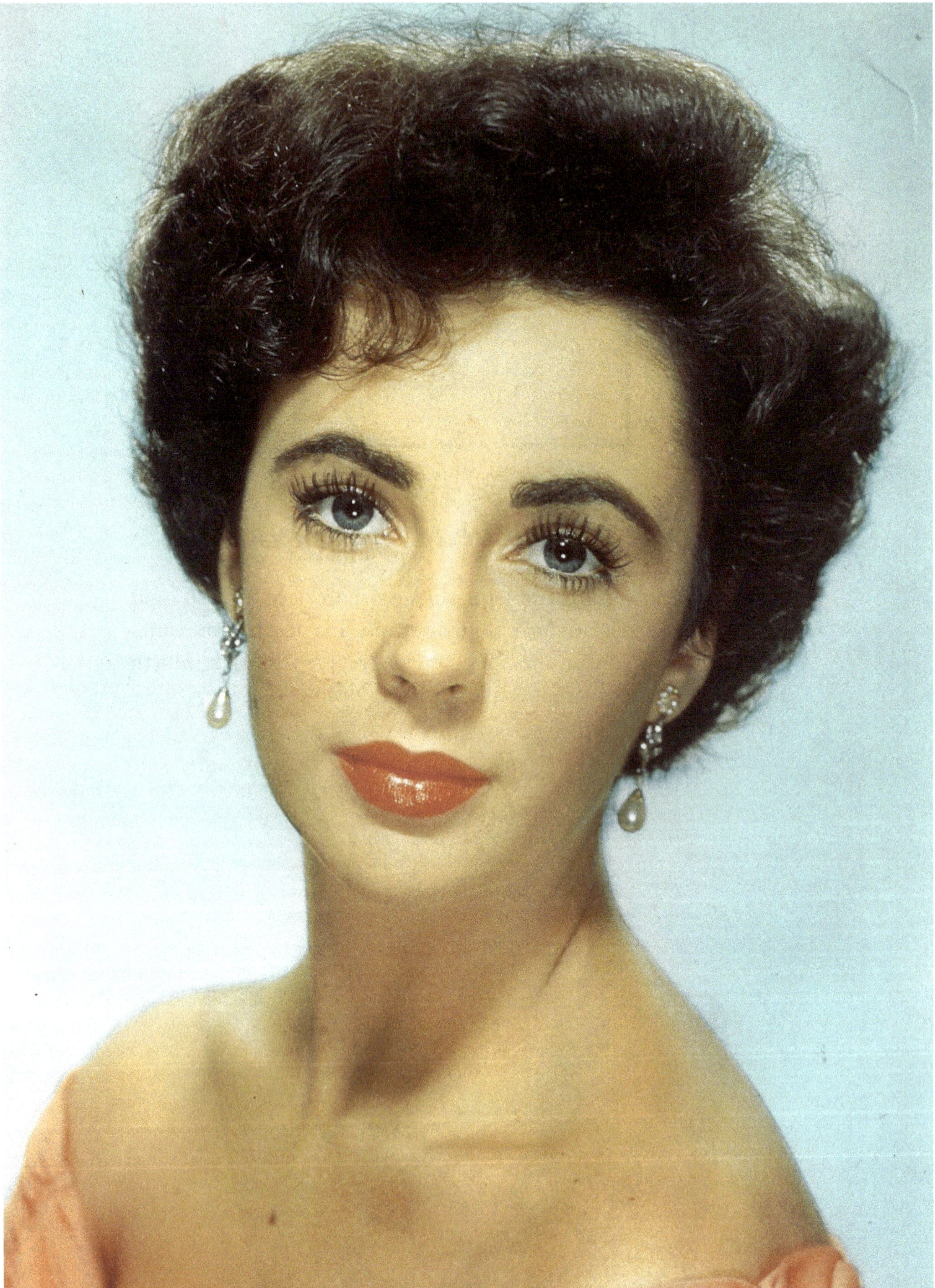

Elizabeth's written hand

Original handwritten letter from Elizabeth to friend Jeannie talking about her new film and trip with her mother to England, 1949.

Source: George Houle books and autographs, New York.

The rose hair clip

This porcelain rose hair clip was once part of Dame Elizabeth Taylor's hair and beauty regime. It is a hand painted hairclip with rose petals and light green rose leaves. The clip is 1.5 inches in diameter.

Source: Roni Howard, MGM pay clerk and personal assistant (1947-1975) to Elizabeth Taylor. Made by Shelley of England.

The hairclip dish

This porcelain hairclip dish was once part of Elizabeth Taylor's hair and beauty regime. It is hand painted with rose petals and light green rose leaves. The dish is 3.45 inches in diameter.

Source: Roni Howard, MGM pay clerk and personal assistant (1947- 1975) to Elizabeth Taylor. Made by Shelley of England.

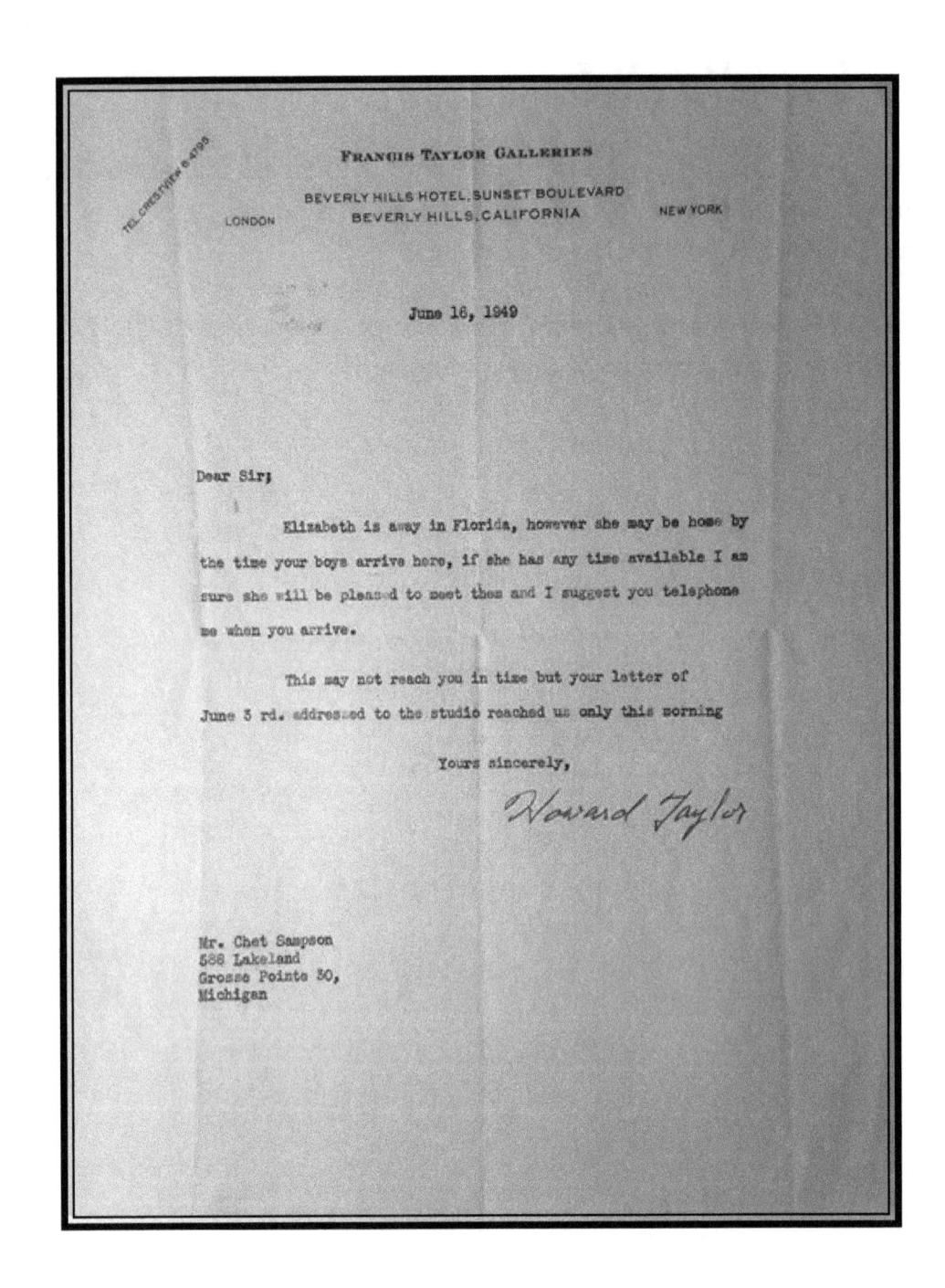

Original Frances Taylor Gallery letterhead paper, on which Elizabeth's brother, Howard sent correspondence on her behalf June 14, 1949.

Source: George Houle books and autographs, Los Angeles, USA.

Elizabeth was now seen as a marketable asset and to coincide with the release of the MGM classic, *Little Women*, the studio put Elizabeth's face to the new line of women's hats.

Source: Movie Goer magazine, 1949.

Original Elizabeth autograph, 1949.

On the Thursday evening of January 26, 1950, Elizabeth graduated from the University High School, West Los Angeles, just short of her 18th birthday. Later that year May 6, 1950, at the Good Sheppard church in Beverly Hills, Elizabeth married her first husband Nicholas Hilton, heir to the Waldorf-Astoria Hotel New York, and the 3000 room Stevens Hotel Chicago.

The publicity surrounding the wedding was a great advertising tool for MGM, who released the Vincente Minnelli film *Father of the Bride* two days later. Actress Jane Powell was Elizabeth's bridesmaid. The marriage of Elizabeth to Nicky was the most sumptuous wedding of the century.

Here, newlyweds Elizabeth and Nicky Hilton greet guests before their departure.

A rarety, Elizabeth Taylor Hilton signature, 1950.

Source: Weekend magazine.

'When you give your daughter away in marriage, you can't possibly give all those memories along with her. Elizabeth no longer looked like a child as she and Nick knelt together. Her face had a new diginity that I'd never seen before.'

- Frances Taylor, 1950.

The Wedding gift

This sterling silver presentation tray was gifted to Elizabeth Taylor and Conrad Hilton Jr as a wedding gift from the former Governor of Florida (1949-1953). The tray is inscribed, "The Hiltons from Gov, and Mrs. Fuller Warren". The verso is stamped "Fisher Sterling". The circular tray has a diameter of 7 inches.

Source: Julien's Auction House California, USA/ Fisher Silversmiths Inc.

47

Pictured is newly wed Elizabeth Hilton with her first husband Nicky, 1950.

Source: Virginia USA.

'There is no sure way of getting the perfect husband - just luck I guess.'

- Elizabeth Taylor

The MGM hand coloured portrait

Original and authentic hand coloured portrait of Elizabeth Taylor promotion the film *A Place in the Sun* 1951. The portrait originated from the corridors of MGM studios California. The portrait hung in the corridors of the MGM studios California. At an MGM auction in the 1970's it was purchased by an Antique dealer. In 1992 Hunter Gatherer Antiques sold the portrait to the collector.

Source: MGM Studios/ Hunter Gatherer.

ELIZABETH TAYLOR
METRO-GOLDWYN-MAYER

The bow head dress

This is a pink diamond shaped netted hair net which is highlighted by a cotton pink bow tie was once owned by Dame Elizabeth Taylor.

Source: Roni Howard estate- personal assistant to Elizabeth Taylor from 1947 to 1972.

The silk head dress

This is a pale blue head wrap/dress with circular fabric panels throughout, which is open at the back and is tied off with two blue ribbons. Appears to have been custom made as it has no size and or label.

Source: Roni Howard estate- personal assistant to Elizabeth Taylor from 1947 to 1972.

It took 15 MGM seamstresses over two months to stitch together Elizabeth's dress, however after their honeymoon aboard the Queen Mary; it was evident that they had both made a big mistake.

Reports of Nicky Hilton's bad temper and alcohol abuse lead to their divorce on February 1, 1951. Irreconcilable differences were cited in the divorce court. In the same year, Elizabeth appeared in the sequel to *Father of the Bride, Father's Little Dividend*. Both films were box office hits for the studio.

Later in the year, she was lent out to Paramount Pictures for the George Stevens black and white classic, *A Place in the Sun*, which was said to be Elizabeth's favourite and one of her best works.

Shortly after the divorce from her first husband Conrad "Nicky" Hilton, Elizabeth Taylor instructed her personal assistant at the time, Roni Howard, to clean out her storage area, and keep anything he wanted. Mr. Howard was employed as Dame Elizabeth's personal assistant from 1947- 1975. On the list of items shipped to this collection was a wedding band, a diamond necklace, and a variety of personal effects, such as lipsticks and hair brushes.

Lipstick No. 1

Northam Warren lipstick in a 24 carat gold plated case (1950s).

Lipstick No 2

Tussy Cosmetics "Contraband" etched fleur-de-lis case. The lipstick is contained in a 24 carat gold plated case (ca 1947).

Source: Lisa Maalouf/ Roni Howard estate.

Tussy Lips
gorgeously red—smooth as satin

No other Lipstick...
has these Exclusive features
Clear Red
Blue Red
Rose Red
3 shades for your coloring
Max Factor - Hollywood

'We were just too young. But you don't know or realise it at the time. A few weeks after the wedding we both discovered we only liked each other, but we had stars in our eyes and believed love would come' – Elizabeth Taylor

The gold hair bush

This handcrafted gold hair brush is believed to have been gifted to Elizabeth Taylor by her mother Sara in the late 1940's. It became one of the many items that personal assistant to Elizabeth Taylor, Roni Howard, saved when asked to clean out a storage area at the Taylor estate.

Source: Lisa Maalouf/ Roni Howard estate.

The hair brush set

This hair brush set was another item saved from the storage clean out.

Source: Lisa Maalouf/ Roni Howard estate.

The hair curlers

These are an assortment of curlers and pins used to beautify Dame Elizabeth Taylor's beautiful locks.

It is believed that they were used between 1947-1974, the same time period that Roni Howard was Elizabeth Taylor's pay clerk and personal assistant. Strands of Elizabeth Taylor's hair are still attached to many of the curlers.

Source: Lisa Maalouf/ Roni Howard estate.

The cotton white gloves

These white cotton gloves originated from the private collection of Sydney Guilaroff. Elizabeth gave Sydney many items from her personal wardrobe over the years that they worked together. These gloves may have well been worn by Elizabeth Taylor while on board the Queen Mary.

Source: Sydney Guilaroff Estate, USA.

The antique rhinestone necklace

Costume jewelry was the beginning of Elizabeth Taylor's lifelong love affair with jewels of all kinds. This 16-inch necklace is encrusted with over 140 rhinestones. It has a draped style motif and was made by Kramer of New York.

Louis Kramer, who started the company in 1943, was later joined by his brothers, Morris and Harry, as he tapped into the burgeoning costume-jewelry market. All aspects of the business took place in New York City, so the pieces were marked "Kramer," "Kramer N.Y.," or "Kramer of New York."

Source: Originally from the personal collection of Gordon Bau. The necklace was then obtained for this collection from Roslyn Herman & Co of New York.

The many brooches

Kramer of New York was a company founded in New York in 1943 by Kramer. The company produced some of the world's leading costume jewelry at the time, using sparkling Austrian crystals. Kramer of New York also used high quality rhinestones.

Kramer marketed its jewelry under a variety of marks including 'Kramer of NY', 'Kramer of NY City', 'Kramer', and when it made jewelry for Christian Dior, 'Christian Dior by Kramer'. Trademarks owned by the company included 'Amourelle', 'Perles De Lune', 'The Diamond Look', 'Dura-Gold', 'KJC' and 'The Golden Look'. Kramer of New York was located 393 5th Avenue, New York, New York.

Although the company ceased operations in 1980, Kramer of New York is still a well-respected costume jewelry name today.

This is a set of two multi-faceted fashion Eisenberg brooches owned and used by Elizabeth Taylor in the early to late 1940's. The words "Eisenberg Original" were used from roughly 1935 to 1945, while just plain "Eisenberg" or "Eisenberg Ice" was used from about 1945 to 1950. The jewelry became as popular as the fashions and by the 1930's the company began producing high quality jewelry using the best Austrian stones to be sold separately from the clothing.

These two "Eisenberg Ice" stamped brooches were made in the mid 1940's and are adorned with Swarovski crystals and coloured stones. Eisenberg clips and / or brooches are usually festooned with aqua, ruby, and crystal stones. Many Eisenberg pieces are abstract and vaguely organic, but others resemble kings, queens, mermaids, ballerina's and in this instance Hollywood Royalty, Dame Elizabeth Taylor.

Source: Rosyn Herman and Co of New York.

This original 1950's fashion jewelry was the beginning of Miss Taylor's lifelong love affair with jewels.

Elizabeth was now earning in excess of $5500 a week and completed two films in 1952, *Love Is Better Than Ever* and the Richard Thorpe production of *Ivanhoe*.

Just one week before Elizabeth's twentieth birthday, she married 39-year-old Michael Wilding (Michael Charles Gauntlet) in a small private reception at Claridge's in London. Elizabeth became pregnant and made only one film in 1953. On January 6, 1953, Michael Howard Wilding was born and soon after was given the name of 'Britches' and Michael, 'the noise', Wilding.

Michael Wilding was against his wife doing more than two films a year, as she was suffering from slight cardiac weakness. An illness that would later develop into heart failure and take her life.

Original autograph from Michael Wilding, 1952.

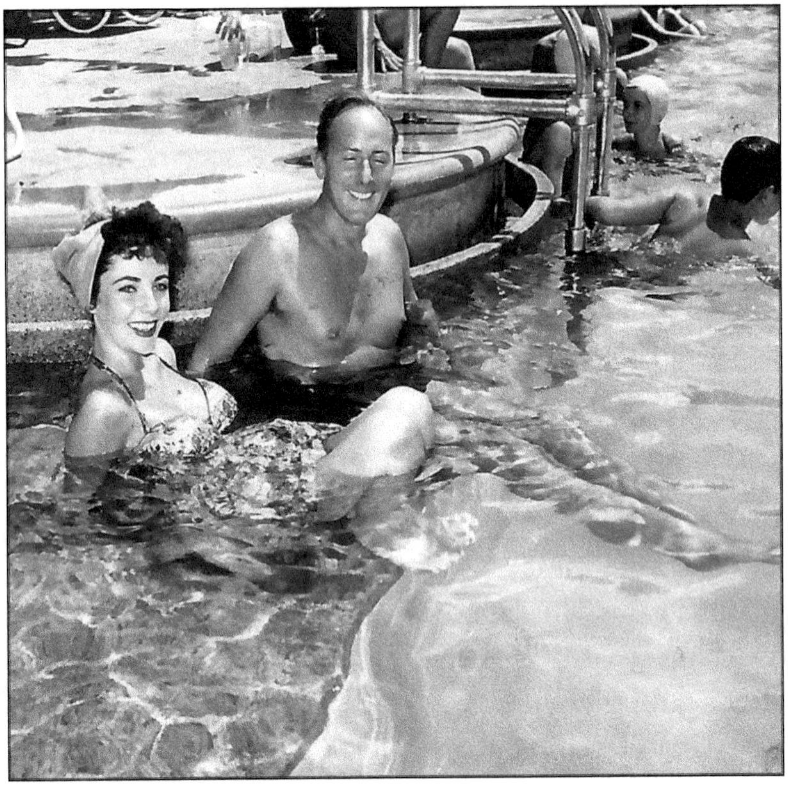

Elizabeth waits at the Los Angeles airport for a flight to England, signed in person, 1953.

Source: Joe Decker.

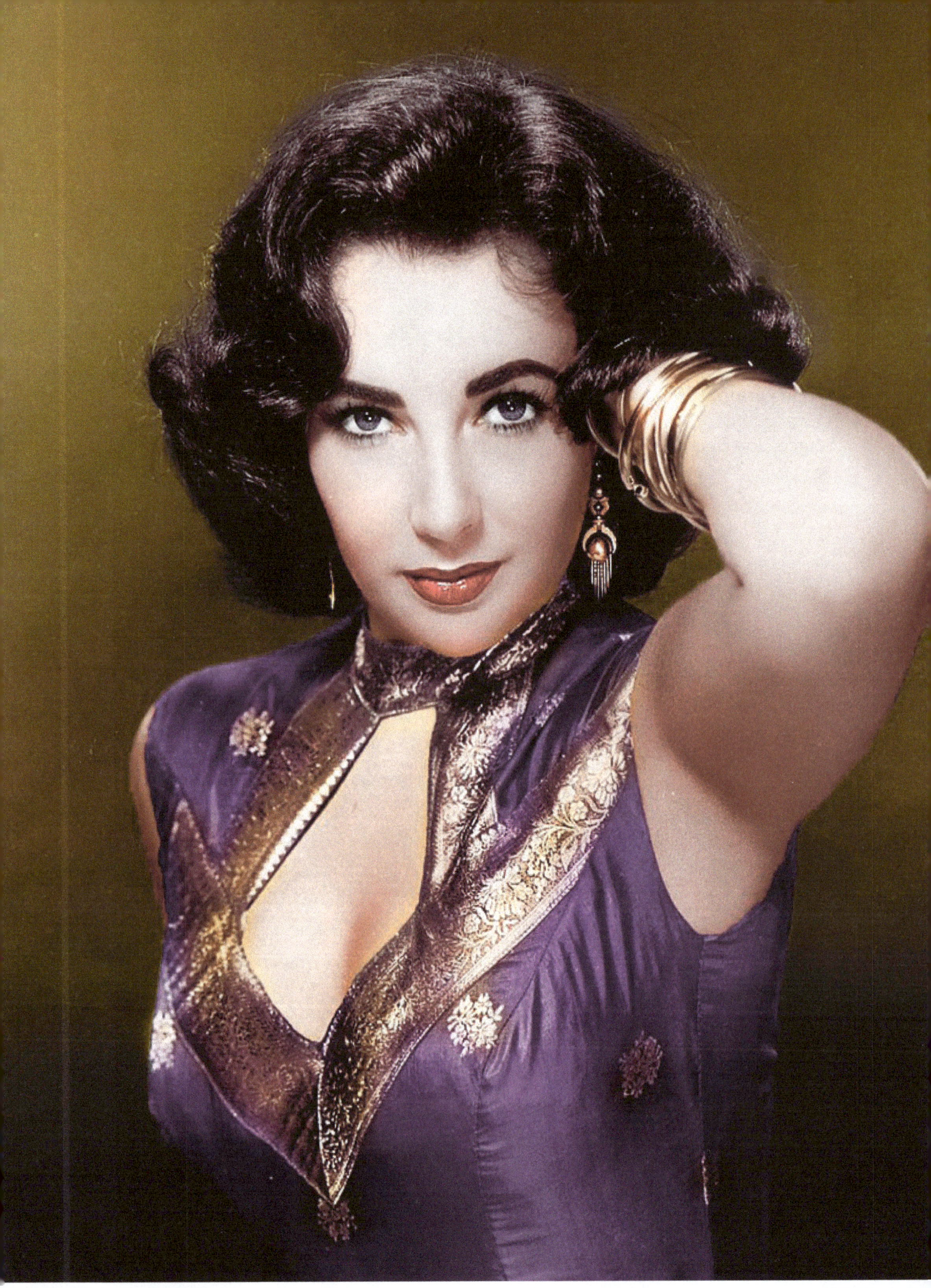

Elizabeth's grandfather, Howard Taylor is pictured here with the US President Dwight D Eisenhower. The two men with their fishing catch combine political history with entertainment, 1953.

Source: Thomas Family, USA.

The Elizabeth Taylor fan club

In 1953, Elizabeth was honorary president of the Elizabeth Taylor Fan Club. Fans like Marilyn Hill received a beautiful collection of images of Elizabeth and a signed membership card from Elizabeth herself.

Through her 70-year career Elizabeth always took time to correspond with her fans, including yours truly.

Source: Marilyn Hill, 1953.

Elizabeth shares a scene with Fernado Lamas a in the film, *The Girl Who had Everything*, 1954.

Source: MGM.

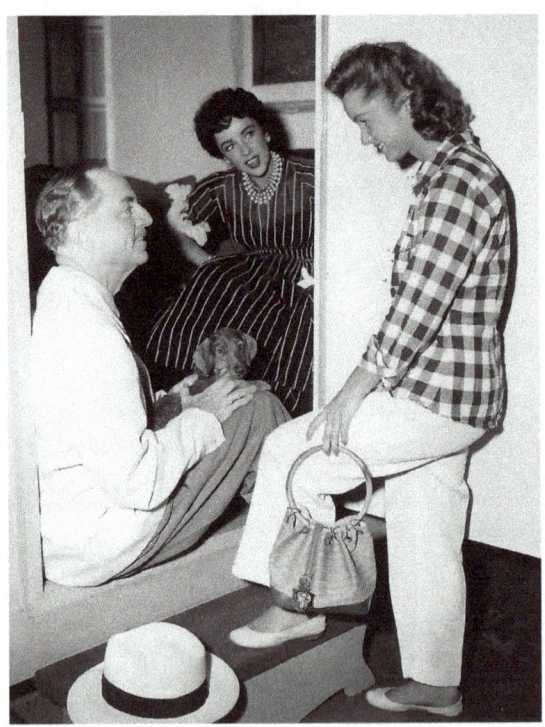

A young Debbie Reynolds visits Elizabeth and co-stars, Gig Young and William Powell on the set of *The Girl Who had Everything*, 1954.

Source: Clarence S Bull Estate, USA.

Though enjoying critical success, Elizabeth was increasingly dissatisfied with the offered roles and after a sequence of indifferent films in 1953, she was eager to return to the silver screen in the William Dieterle film *Elephant Walk*, 1954.

This was a film first designed for her, however still pregnant with her second child, Christopher, Elizabeth was forced to turn down the role and Vivien Leigh who bore a striking resemblance to Elizabeth was sent to Ceylon to begin shooting. But this did not work out and Elizabeth reclaimed the role. The book store scene at the beginning of *Elephant Walk* shows a female attendant, played by Vivien Leigh.

This is an original *Elephant Walk* day bill, 1954.

Source: MGM.

The Last Time I saw Paris screen worn wig

This wig was worn by Dame Elizabeth Taylor in her role as Helen Ellswirth in the 1954 romantic drama, *The Last Time I saw Paris*.

This short brown wig, made from real human hair and includes original hairpins, storage box, and wig stock record. An amazing piece of Hollywood history. In her role as Helen, Dame Elizabeth got caught out in the rain and developed pneumonia and died in the film.

Source: MGM Wig Works/ MGM movie and memorabilia Auction in 1974 / Heritage Auctions Texas.

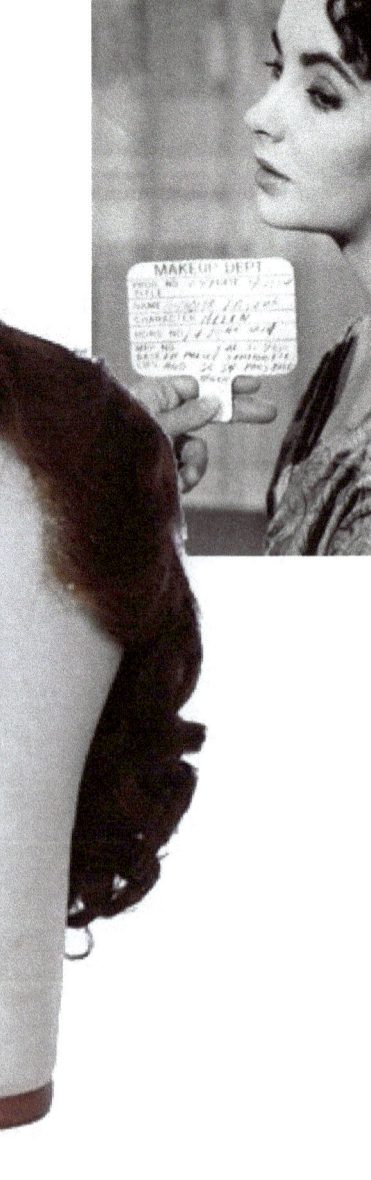

> *Elizabeth Taylor*
> *Hollywood, Calif.*
>
> March 24, 1955
>
> Dear Claire,
>
> Thank you so much for the lovely, little pink kimona.
>
> Both Michael and I think it is so cute, and we can't wait to see it on Christopher!
>
> It was so very thoughtful of you to send such a nice gift, and I do appreciate your kindness.
>
> Sincerely,
>
> *Elizabeth Taylor*
>
> ET/js

Elizabeth and Michael receive a lovely gift for newly born Christopher from a fan by the name of Claire, 1955.

Source: Harmonie Collectables, USA.

Completing, *Rhapsody, Beau Brummell* and *The Last time I Saw Paris* in twelve months and pregnant with her second child, Elizabeth was exhausted but still sought more substantial work. Christopher Edward Wilding was born on February 27, 1955.

Elizabeth now 23 years of age with two children and twenty-five films to her credit, had lost her childhood to Hollywood and now it seemed there was no going back. While considered to be the greatest beauty of her generation, no-one, critics, herself and fans alike were convinced she was a great actress.

In later years, Dame Elizabeth would become more famous for being an activist for human equality, compassion and HIV Aids awareness.

At 23, Elizabeth was indeed the most beautiful woman in America, if not, the world.

Elizabeth entered motherhood stage and did not return to the silver screen until early 1956, in the film *Giant*.

Source: Culver Pictures.

' Having children didn't change Elizabeth, it broadened her; she didn't get dressed up, she used to just slob around.'

– Liz Smith/columnist

Elizabeth returned to work as Lesley Benedict, in the George Stevens film, *Giant*, based on Edna Ferber's bestselling novel, also co-starring Rock Hudson (Roy Harold Fitzgerald) and James Dean (James Byron Dean). This film would see Elizabeth's character age over 50 years, earning her $175,000 and win George Stevens an Academy Award for his direction of this Texan family dynasty drama. During the filming, 24-year-old James Dean died in a car accident. *Giant* was only his third film and Elizabeth was devastated by the loss. It is believed that James Dean left a party at Elizabeth's home and was going too fast to take a bend and collided with a tree.

Pictured is Elizabeth enjoying watermelon with her co-stars on the set of *Giant*, 1956 and the original draft from the film, signed by Elizabeth, Rock Hudson and James Dean. 1955.

Source: Fred Guiol and Ivan Moffat.

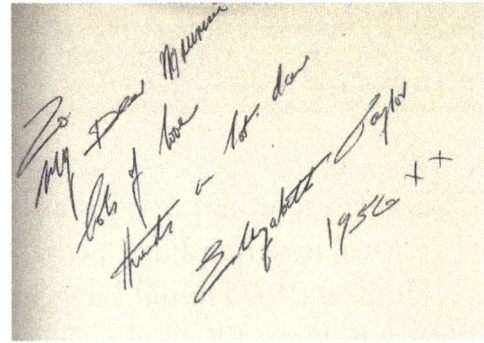

A personal autograph was obtained from Elizabeth when she stayed at the Waldorf Astoria Beverly Hills during the premiere of *Giant*, in 1956. Elizabeth radiates with beauty in this candid unseen image. Here she is seen at the world premiere of George Stevens' production of *Giant* at the Roxy theatre, West Hollywood, a benefit for the Muscular Dystrophy Association of America.

Source: Edgar Vash/Barry Taub and Waldorf doorman at the time, 'Maurice.'

Elizabeth's role as Lesley Benedict in *Giant* is captured in these unique celebrity dolls.

Source: Franklin Mint.

ELISABETH TAYLOR

Elizabeth was knocking critics dead as a serious adult actress and so began her ten-year reign. With her next film, directed by Edward Dmtryk, *Raintree County*, and her newly found maturity and power, Elizabeth received her very first Academy Award nomination and was given her star on the Hollywood walk of fame.

While all this was a great turn around for America's favourite girl, her marriage to Michael Wilding was wavering and on January 30, 1957. Elizabeth was divorced for the second time.

All her adult life it would appear that Elizabeth longed for a father figure. She was looking for love and found it in the arms of 45-year-old, Mike Todd (Avron Hirsch Goldbogen). It was Todd's third marriage, his first wife Bertha Freshman died and his second marriage to Joan Blondell ended in divorce. Mike Todd married Elizabeth at Puerto Marques, a tiny village near Acapulco on February 2, 1957. Armed Mexican troops kept reporters and tourists away, while the couple said, 'Si' in the Spanish civil ceremony.

Mike presented his violet-eyed ravened haired bride with a diamond-studded bracelet, earrings and ring set, valued at $87,000. Singer Eddie Fisher was best man and Debbie Reynolds was matron of honour.

Pictured is Elizabeth's very own plaque on the Hollywood Walk of Fame at 6336 Hollywood Boulevard, California, USA.

Raintree County screen worn crinoline

This is an original hoop dress produced as part of the costumes designed by Walter Plunkett for the MGM classic, *Raintree County*, 1956. Dame Elizabeth Taylor is seen wearing the hoop dress if not a similar one in an opening scene, where she is having her portrait taken.

The hoop dress has a colour swat that indicates which dress it is to be worn under. It is worn under the dark red dress in the scene where Elizabeth Taylor frantically throws her childhood dolls against a wall and smashes them and their dark secret. The hoop dress is made of bamboo hoops, the lace and tulle is nylon.

Elizabeth Taylor and the scene number is hand-written on the waistband. The dress came accompanied also with a handwritten sign that indicates that it was not to be hired out as it was worn by Elizabeth Taylor. The dress took a worldwide tour before finding its way to Australia and to this collection. A bittersweet experience for Angela Schneider at Tindsel and Stars, who gained peace of mind in knowing the dress's final resting place was here in the Elizabeth Taylor collection.

The fabric for the crinoline is made from marquisette. The corset/ bodice is made of coutil. After filming the Crinoline was stored at the MGM studios until it was purchased at a 1970's sale by Barbara Awerkamp.

Source: Angela Schneider at Tindsel and Stars Los Angeles, CA. It was purchased from Angela In 2017, for this collection.

' I can grow with Mike.'
- Elizabeth Taylor

Front

Elizabeth Taylor "Raintree County"

Elizabeth Taylor "Raintree County"

Back

The Raintree County Picnic

Antique Picnic Basket and Accessories

This picnic basket was often filled with snacks that were shared on many occasions, with some of the cast of the movie classic, *Raintree County*, 1957. The picnic basket contains several little baskets/ lids, one with feathers on top. Two ladies' handkerchiefs w/ horse head. Antique German dessert plates (with fruits or vegetables and gold trim). Also enclosed is a set of six mother of pearl-handled knives in a felt roll tie, antique silver salt/ pepper/seasoning glass w/ silver.

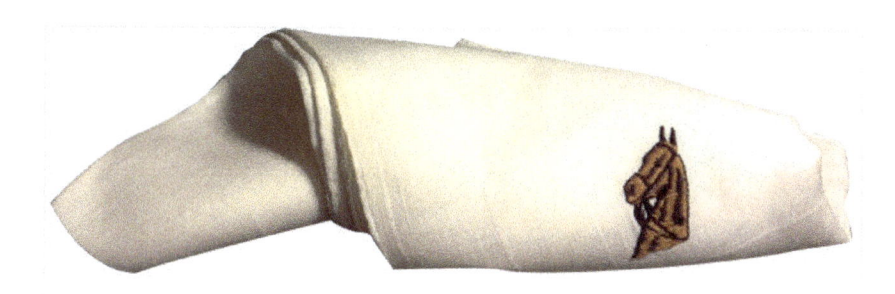

The antique silver salt/pepper/seasoning glass w/ silver was made by Wilcox International Silver Co. The set of six pearl-handled knives in a felt roll was made by the Meriden Cutlery Co 1366.

Barbara Burgin Leigh was a fan of Elizabeth Taylor and the film, *Raintree County*. She told her daughter Jamie that this basket and the items inside were used to share lunch with the stars and crew during breaks in filming.

There is also a quilt that Barbara would take with her to use as a picnic blanket. Light blue and white, Jacobs Ladder pattern. Barbara's sister Mary Lucille Burgin (born in 1900) hand made this quilt in the 1940's during WW11. The cast of *Raintree County* used it for picnic lunches. It is an antique and was used, as you can tell by the wear depicted in the photo.

The blueliner in the basket was made by my Barbara Burgin Leigh. Barbara Burgin Leigh didn't take any photos. She said they weren't thinking of photos at the time, they just wanted the experience of being there.

Barbara often talked of Elizabeth Taylor, Eva Marie Saint, Montgomery Clift, and Lee Marvin all gathering with them for lunch or snacks during breaks in shooting. She said Elizabeth and Eva Marie were both very demure and kind. Lee Marvin was a jokester, and Montgomery Clift was still recovering from the automobile accident he had been involved in before the Kentucky shoot could conclude. She said she did not witness it, but heard that Elizabeth Taylor & Mr. Clift (who was from Louisville) would skinny dip in Dix River.

When contacted in 2017, Eva Marie Saint remembers the picnics on the Kentucky River.

Source: Jamie Leigh. Item purchased for this collection before an estate sale in 2013.

The watch pendant

A dainty & feminine Ernst and Carl Eduard Bucherer Swiss pendant watch with 24 carat gold 32" chain was worn by Elizabeth Taylor off set whilst filming *Raintree County* in Central Kentucky 1956.

Elizabeth Taylor gifted the item to Thelma, a friend of Barbara Brandt Burgin Leigh. Barbara and Thelma prepared a picnic basket each day and Elizabeth Taylor would, on occasion, join them on the banks of the Dix River Lincoln County.

The case is 2.5cm in diameter and decorated in enamel with pink & green floral & leaf motif. Each chain segment is approx. 1/2" long with a circle at each end, joined to the next link with two small rings.

When Barbara Brandt Burgin Leigh passed her daughter Jamie Leigh sold it to the collection in 2013.

Source: Jamie Leigh. Item purchased for this collection before an estate sale in 2013.

Pictured here is little James (Jim) Burgin Leigh with Welby Burgin (Uncle) playing on the train on the set of *Raintree Country* 1956. The real train, century-old locomotion is the biggest prop and is hauled cross country on its own flat car from a Baltimore museum. In another picture, you can see Barbara (Bob) Brandt Burgin Leigh in her nurse uniform 1948. Barbara had this pendant stored in a bank safe at the Lincoln County National Bank accompanied by a note to her family declaring the item belonged to Elizabeth Taylor.

Elizabeth Taylor is pictured relaxing and signing autographs off set during the filming of *Raintree County*. Pictured also is an authentic signed *Raintree County* post card which could have been something Barbara Brand Burgin Leigh may have also acquired during her experience in meeting and picnicking with Elizabeth Taylor and the crew. Examples of Elizabeth Taylor and Eva Marie Saint's autographs obtained during the same timeline are pictures last.

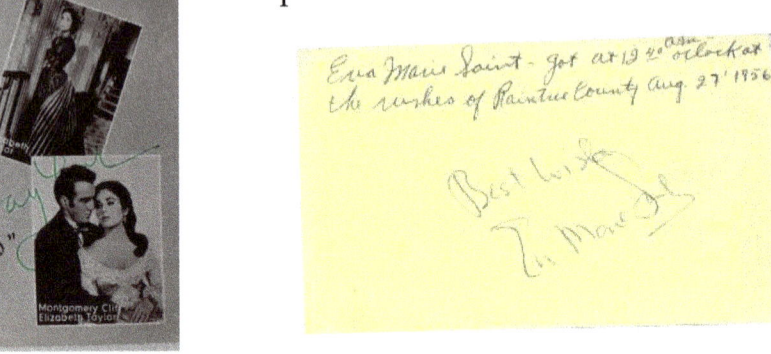

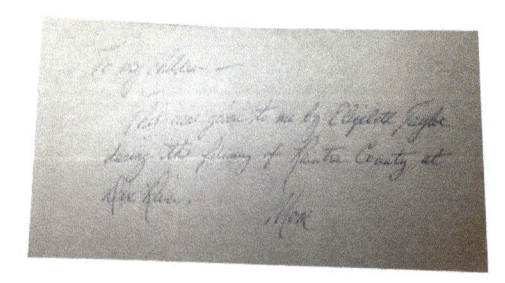

90

The embellished silver bracelet

The bracelet is 10cm in diameter and is structured with small embellished silver panels that link together with eight silver leaves like links. Sterling silver safety chain ensures a secure fit.

Source: Jamie Leigh. Item purchased for this collection before an estate sale in 2013.

The Raintree dinner party

This beautiful blue velvet hat, hat box, 17-inch princess string of pearls, fold away ashtray and hat pins have been stored away by Edward Parkes since they were first gifted to his wife Sallie by Dame Elizabeth Taylor, on the set of *Raintree County* in 1957.

In 1956, Edward Parkes was having dinner with his soon-to-be wife, Sallie, at Beaumont Inn in Harrodsburg, Kentucky. Edward glanced across the room to see an old World War II buddy….it was actor Lee Marvin, who was in the area for the filming of *Raintree County*.

Mr. Parkes said to Sallie, "Well, there's my old buddy, Lee Marvin." Sallie was most skeptical, saying, "Yeah, right." Edward immediately took her by the hand and walked over to the table. Marvin recognized Edward right away, standing to shake his hand and give him a bear hug. Edward then introduced Sallie to Marvin. The men reminisced about old times, while Sallie stood in awe. Before parting ways for the evening, Marvin invited them to the film set.

The following week, Edward and Sallie journeyed to the film set, where Marvin introduced his wartime pal to the cast. Sallie, quite classy as Edward described, was taken with the whole experience. During filming, they would visit the set on numerous occasions. They were also invited to private dinner parties as Marvin's guests, where they became rather familiar with the cast members.

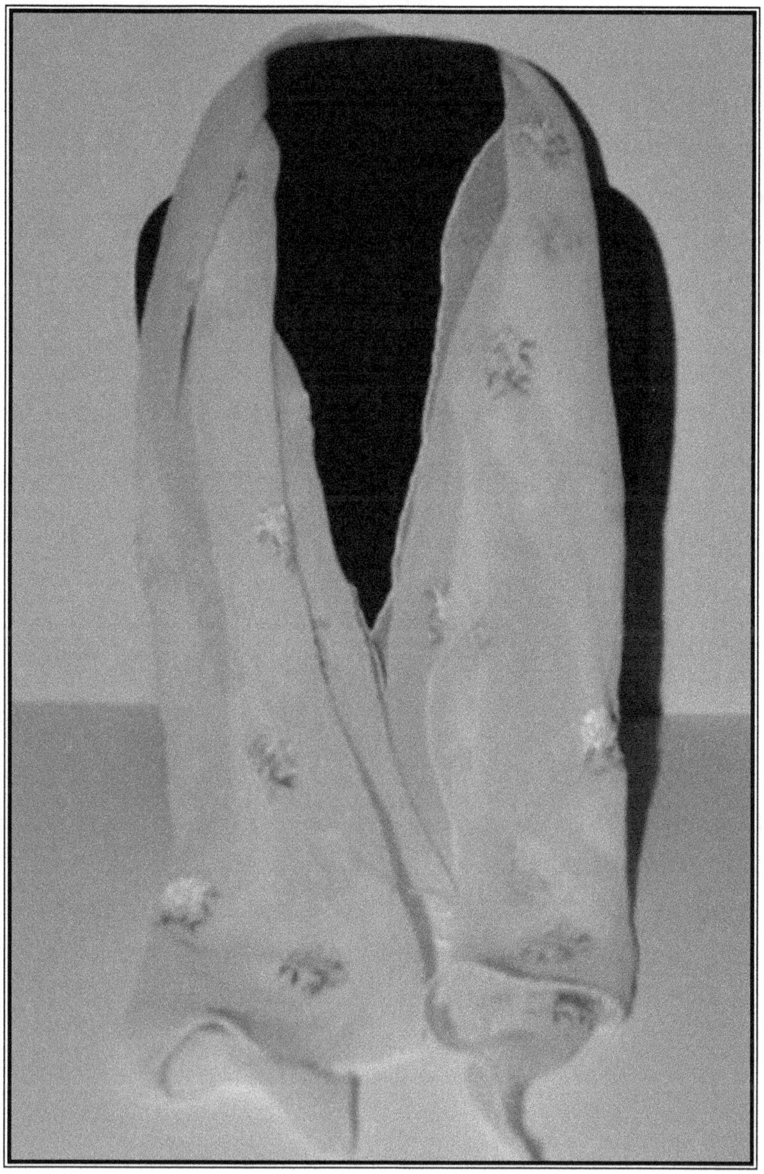

Edward said Sallie was very taken with the actors and actresses, but was especially enamored with Elizabeth Taylor. Edward said Ms. Taylor sensed Sallie's admiration and before the filming wrapped, she gave Sallie rather nice keepsakes.....a beautiful Navy velvet hat with pearls, in its box, and a string of pearls.

The *Raintree County* story and providence were first established through meeting daughter to Barbara Brandt Leigh, Jamie, who passed on her mother's Raintree County story and artefacts to this collection. So to establish the providence with these items, it is said that Jamie's husband was once the carer to Mrs. Sallie Parkes and that is how their acquaintance was first established. Through the years and after the passing of Mrs. Sallie Parke, Jamie and her husband remained in contact with Edward Parkes, hence the story of how these items came to be.

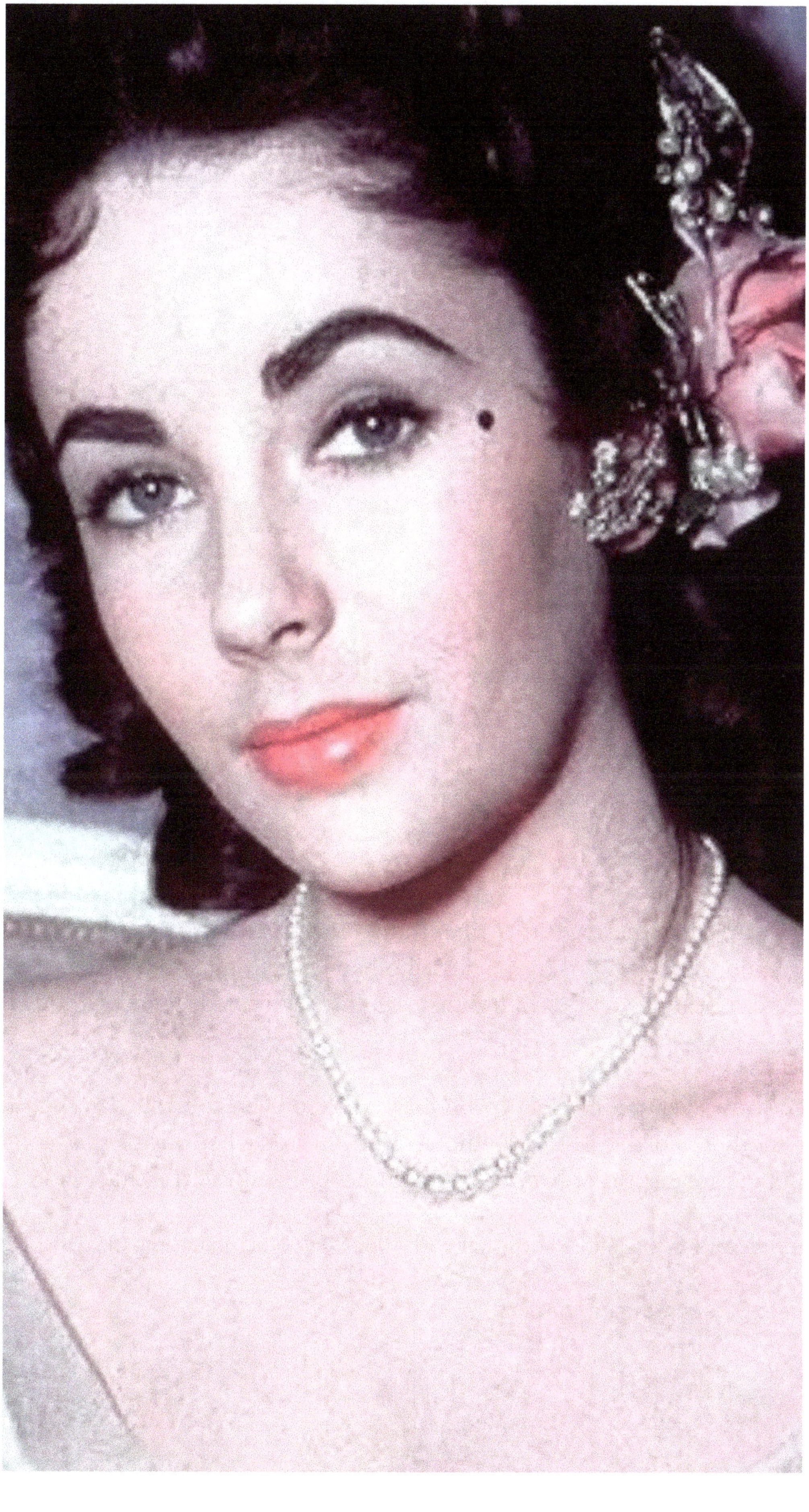

Dear Mr. Ferrari:

Thank you for the fruit and baby food. Baby Liza, mother and Daddy are enjoying it.

Sincerely,

Elizabeth & Michael Todd

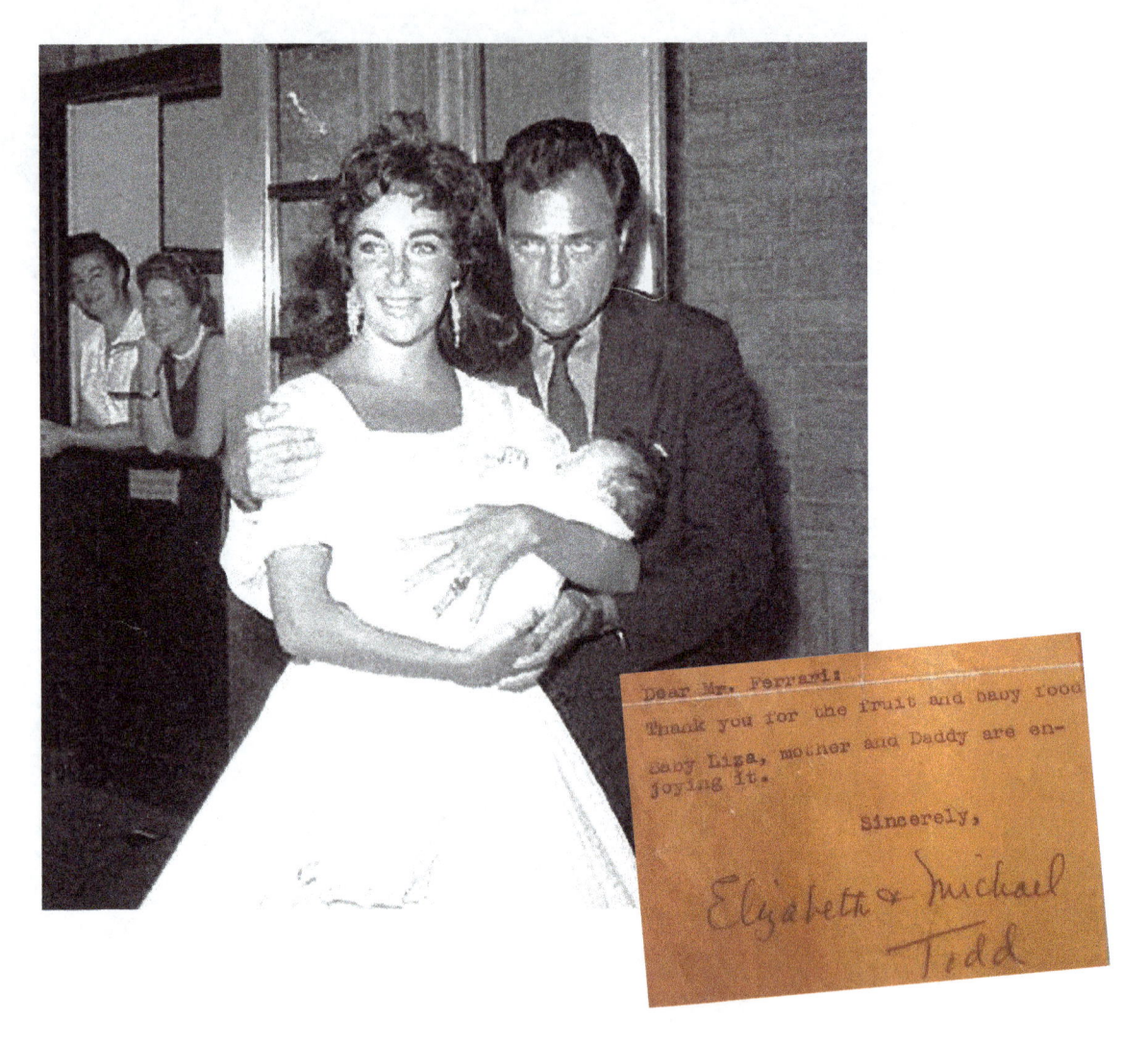

During her marriage to Mike Todd, Elizabeth had transformed from the poor little rich girl to the girl who had everything and on August 6, 1957, Elizabeth gave birth to her first daughter, Elizabeth Frances Todd, (known as Liza).

Mike Todd liberated Elizabeth who for years had been controlled and dominated by her mother and the MGM studio system. He took her out of that controlling environment to a world of her own, full of freedom and excitement.

Elizabeth and Mike left the hospital with their new born daughter Liza Todd, 1957.

Source: Screen Stars magazine.

Mike Todd is embraced by his wife while he reflects on his life after winning an Academy Award for his film, *Around The World In 80 Days*, which grossed over 17 million dollars at the box office.

' I've fallen in love for the first time.'

- Elizabeth Taylor

'When receiving the award, Mike said, 'I can't believe it, to win two of the biggest prizes in one year, the academy award and my darling wife, Elizabeth. I must be the luckiest man alive' – Mike Todd

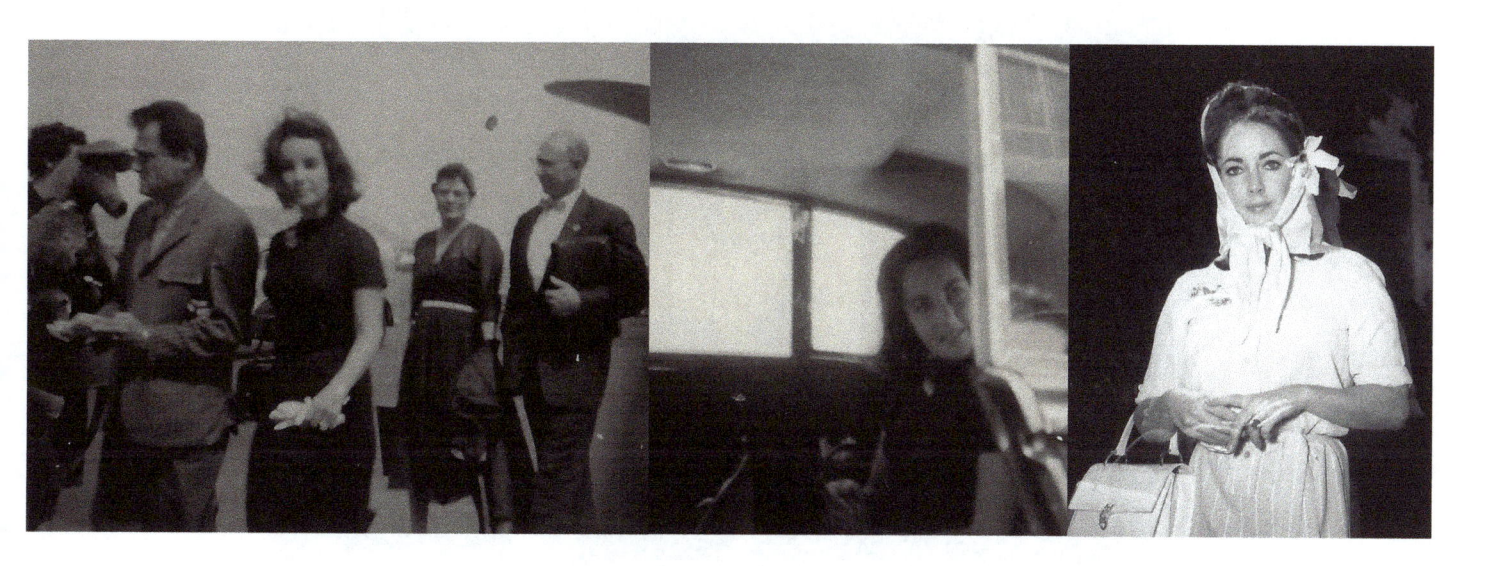

Elizabeth in Australia

Touring parts of the world to promote, *Around The World In 80 Days*, the Todds arrived in Melbourne, Australia on November 7, 1957, after a 26-hour flight and stayed at the Menzies Hotel, where they were mobbed by over 800 fans.

The following day, Mike Todd and film star wife Elizabeth presented a cheque for 14,171 pounds to the Lord Mayor Cr Thomas at the town hall. On their departure some days later a fan by the name of Peter Tremayne gave Elizabeth a three foot six-inch kangaroo, made from real kangaroo skin.

The Todds' at Ascot in Syndey, Australia, 1957.

Source: Unknown, candid snapshot of Elizabeth when on tour in Australia, 1957.

Elizabeth Taylor and husband Mike Todd attended Regent theatre Melbourne, Australia

Source: Philip Hartley.

Double-Breasted Herringbone Coat

This blended woolen double breasted coat was owned and worn by Dame Elizabeth Taylor in the late 1950's. This is a cream silk/wool blend double-breasted coat with a herringbone weave and pearlized buttons. A label reads dejue Paris.

Elizabeth Taylor is pictured wearing a similar styled coat that helps create a good comparison to the one listed.

Source: Julien's Celebrity Auctions in Beverly Hills/ Michael and Fredericka Lam, the founders of The Great American Doll Company.

102

The green crystal pin brooch

This elegant lime green Austrian Swarovski Crystal pin brooch was made in Australia and purchased for Dame Elizabeth Taylor by her then-husband Mike Todd when she made a one-time visit promoting Todd's film, *Around the World in 80 Days*, in 1957.

Source: Sourced from Disneyland Parks and Resorts, Florida.

At 10:41pm on the night of March 21, 1958, the twin-engine lockheed Lodestar called, 'The Liz' climbed to over 1300 feet, only seconds later to crash over the Zuri mountains of New Mexico. After a marriage of only 413 thrilling days, Mike Todd (50), his biographer Art Cohen (49) and pilots, William Verner (45) and Tom Barclay (34) were killed instantly.

On Tuesday, March 25, 1958, Elizabeth was escorted from her car to the graveside by her brother Howard Taylor and her physician Dr Frexford Kennemer. Elizabeth broke free from her escorts and threw herself on her husband's grave, sobbing with grief. While no eulogy was permitted at the Jewish service at Walheim cemetery, Michael Todd junior (29) spoke briefly and movingly of his late father.

The death of Mike Todd made the front page news.

Source: Daily New paper, Perth, Western Australia.

Elizabeth Taylor responds to a letter of condolence regarding the sad loss of husband, Mike Todd.

Elizabeth sheds a tear as she leaves Mike Todd's gravesite, 1958.

Source: United Press International.

After Mike Todd's death, something liberated in Elizabeth and her scorching performance of Maggie the cat, in her next film, *Cat on a Hot Tin Roof*, earned the actress her second Academy Award nomination. As Elizabeth continued to cling to the memories and ghost of her late husband, she found consolation in the arms of then-husband of Debbie Reynolds, Eddie Fisher. A mere seven months after the death of Mike Todd, Elizabeth married Eddie Fisher (Edwin John Fisher) on May 12, 1959.

Wearing a green wedding dress, Elizabeth arrived 18 minutes late for the 15-minute sundown ceremony, which was held at the Beth Shalom Jewish temple in Los Angeles. It was at this time that Elizabeth converted to Judaism and provided a climax to filmland's most sensational love triangle.

Debbie Reynolds consoles good friend Elizabeth Taylor, 1958.

Source: Mexico/Daily New, Australia.

The clear crystal perfume bottle

This clear crystal bottle was given to Dame Elizabeth Taylor from then-husband Mike Todd, who died in a plane crash in Mexico on March 21, 1958. As a part of her grieving process, she was advised by her physician Rex Kennamer to remove any artifacts given to her by Mike.

So in doing so, Elizabeth informed her personal assistant Roni Howard (at the time) to clean away her storage area. He said he was told by Elizabeth Taylor to put aside anything he wanted. So he kept many personal Elizabeth Taylor items until his passing in 2009.

Source: Lisa Maalouf/ Roni Howard estate.

At the time of Mike Todd's death, they were both residing at 1330 Schuyder Drive, Beverly Hills, California. The Picture is the day of Mike Todd's death and an image of the house today. This is the house where Elizabeth's payroll assistant was instructed to clear out unwanted items stored in the garage of the property.

The wedding gown

This wedding gown was delivered to Celebrity Seconds (a memorabilia store) by an unknown person. At the time it was labelled Eddie Fisher. This item is believed to have come from the estate of Eddie Fisher. It is labelled Lula. Lula is one of the world's leading brands of Bridal and Evening wear. This Wedding gown is made of satin. The neckline and shoulders are embellished with floral patterned lace and small pearl buttons. The sleeves are also embellished with a quarter length lace and button up on the sides with several pearl buttons.

Whilst this is not the gown Dame Elizabeth Taylor wore to the wedding of her third husband Eddie Fisher, it could be assumed that it was one that was considered at the time and put to the side, given that it was in the possession of the Eddie Fisher estate when he passed away in September of 2010.

Elizabeth Taylor is pictured here wearing a similar style wedding gown in her role as Kay Banks in the 1950's black and white classic, *Father of the Bride*.

Source: Celebrity Seconds/ Eddie Fisher estate.

Crystal Jewelry Dish

This is a small five-inch diameter crystal dish with a lid and a diamond shape embellishments. The dish contains a few loose crystals, diamonds and rubies that are believed to have originated from the jewelry Dame Elizabeth Taylor housed in the crystal jewelry box when in her possession. This item was **gifted to Elizabeth Taylor from Debbie Reynolds as a wedding present** when she married Eddie Fisher.

Source: Roni Howard, Elizabeth Taylor's pay- clerk 1947-1972.

The set of vases

These three vases are a matching set of four. They were said to be originally gifted to Elizabeth Taylor from husband Mike Todd. The largest of the four vases was kept and later gifted by Elizabeth Taylor to her movie double Michelle Breeze.

Source: Lisa Maalouf/ Roni Howard estate.

It was said that Elizabeth developed a stutter after the sudden death of Mike Todd, but luckily it disappeared on the set. This is a personally signed image of Elizabeth on the set of *Cat on a Hot Tin Roof*.

Also pictured is an original porcelain tribute to Elizabeth's role in *Cat On a Hot Tin Roof*, 1958.

Source: Screen starts magazine/MGM.

Suddenly Last Summer, would be her second film with Montogomery Clift and her first co-starring opposite, Katherine Hepburn. Because of the films shocking subject matter, (cannibalism, homosexuality, and insanity), Elizabeth was strongly advised not to do the film, however, it wound up being a great decision, as both Hepburn and Taylor scored Academy Award nominations in 1959.

Elizabeth's sexually charged portrayal in *Suddenly Last Summer*, eclipsed Marilyn Monroe's and *Suddenly Last Summer* gave Elizabeth her third Academy Award nomination and her very first Golden Globe Award.

After winning her first Golden Globe Award, Elizabeth made two films in 1960, the uncredited role in the Jack Cardiff film, *The Scent of Mystery* and the role of Gloria in the Daniel Mann production of *Butterfield 8*. A role that required Elizabeth to play a prostitute, which was met with her disapproval, she did not want to do the film. Her role was immortalised by Tri-Star and MGM in the form of yet another celebrity doll.

The black lycra elbow length gloves

This pair of ladies black elbow length gloves were once the personal property of Dame Elizabeth Taylor. The gloves have no manufacturer information and are made from a black coated fabric.

Elizabeth Taylor has been seen in similar gloves signing her *Cleopatra* contract, attending galas with then-husband Mike Todd, and also wearing them in her role as "Gloria" in the 1960's film, *Butterfield 8*.

Source: Hollywood Props.

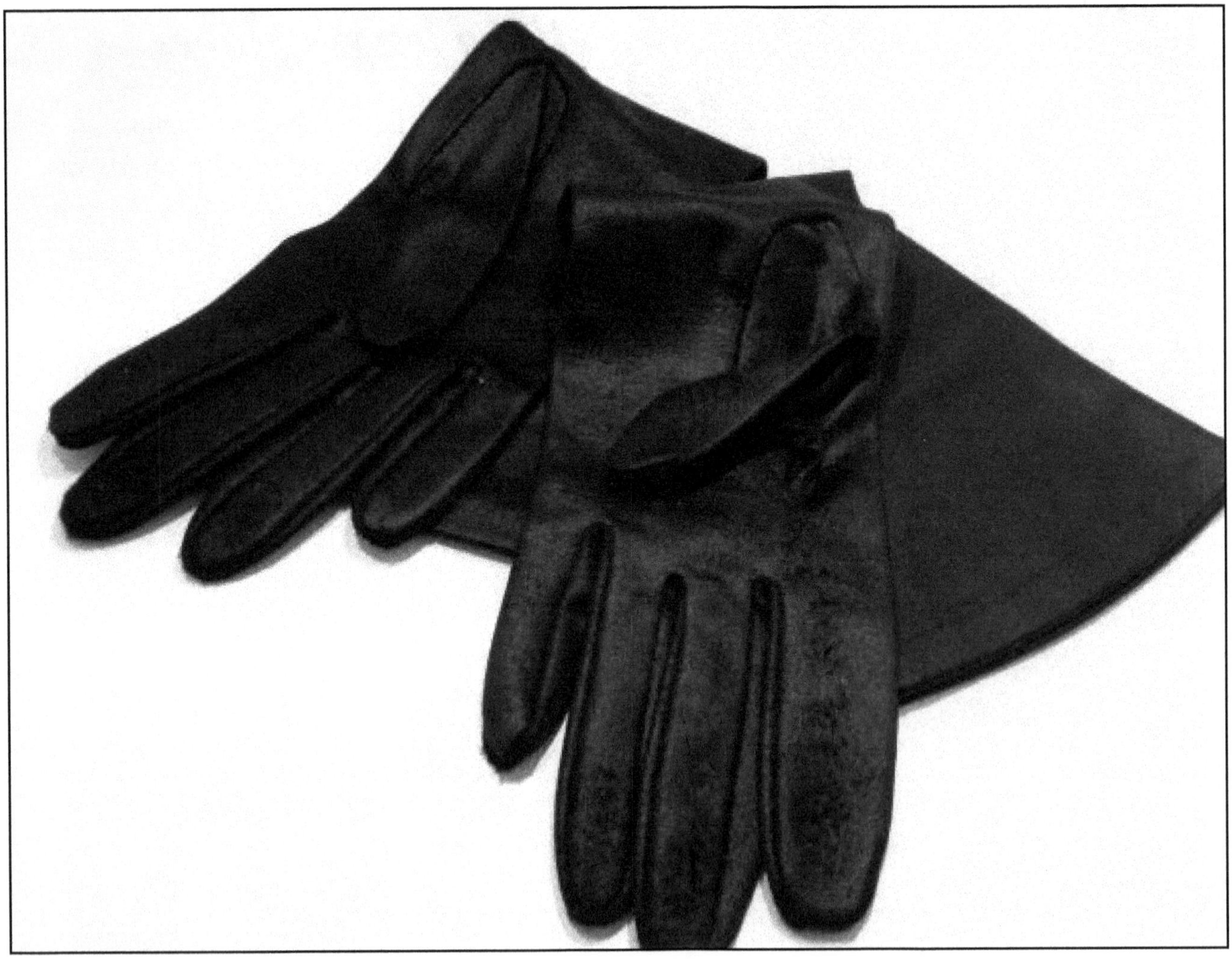

Another celebrity doll replicates the likeness of Elizabeth in her role as Gloria in *Butterfield 8*, 1960.

Source: Tri-Star/MGM.

Elizabeth is pictured here accompanied by gossip columnist Hedda Hopper, as they make their way to Maxim's restaurant, Paris 27, November 1960.

This is a very rare and exclusive 'one off' candid shot of Elizabeth, taken through the limousine window by an adoring fan.

The faux poodle jacket / cape

This silver grey faux poodle fur cape/ jacket is lined with silver satin. It was originally gifted from Dame Elizabeth Taylor to her longtime hairdresser Sydney Guilaroff.

Guilaroff worked with Dame Elizabeth on many films through the 1960's and mid 70's.

The photograph below demonstrates Elizabeth Taylor's likeness for jackets of the same style.

Source: Sydney Guilaroff estate 1995.

During the filming of *Butterfield 8* Elizabeth developed a severe bout of pnemonia, an illness first detected a week before Mike Todd's death. The world that had denounced her as a homewrecker watched for her survival and public sympathy turned *Butterfield 8* into a box office smash, and a fourth Academy nomination. On April 18, 1961, and still recovering from her pneumonia and accompanied by her husband Eddie Fisher, Elizabeth accepts her first Best Actress Academy Award.

Elizabeth's paycheque for her performance in *Butterfield 8* was a little over $150,000, no wonder she thought that asking for one million dollars to do *Cleopatra*, which would be her next film, would be met with laughter. This was not so, even though winning the Oscar had seemed like a consolation prize for not dying from pneumonia, it was also evidence that Elizabeth was now being considered as a talented actress and not just a movie star.

Twentieth Fox studios accepted Elizabeth's fee of one million dollars and several months after her collapse and tracheostomy operation she commenced work on the set of *Cleopatra* and was introduced to her co-star, Welsh actor Richard Burton (Richard Walter Jenkins) who was 37 at the time and whom she felt an instant attraction to and became emotionally attached. For Elizabeth, Richard Burton was a challenge, an irresistible temptation and it was not long before the world was spread with news of yet another adulterous love affair, this time between Elizabeth and Richard Burton. Critics attacked the couple, paparazzi snapped picture after picture and *Cleopatra* became the very first tabloid film and by the end of 1963, Elizabeth and Richard were everywhere. They had symbolised adultress love that was now celebrated.

Cleopatra the legendary Egyptian queen has been portrayed on the silver screen many times before. In 1917, Theda Bara brought *Cleopatra* to life, then Cecil B Demille gave us Claudette Colbert in his 1934 version and in 1945, Vivien Leigh played the queen. MGM's attempt to provide a celluloid classic would also prove costly. Scheduled for a 16-week shoot, the production actually took three years, and despite the huge amount of pre-publicity, Walter Wanger's *Cleopatra* ended up costing 44 million dollars, in today's world, that's equivalent to 340 million.

Elizabeth, then 31 years old was paid her one million, plus 7% of the takings. She took home a staggering 7.6 million dollars and became the very first woman in movie-making history to be paid over one million. *Cleopatra* premiered in New York on June 12, 1963, and ticket sales sold out for four months.

The Vintage Brooch

A circular style brooch with small copper like leaves, highlighted with many small purple, blue and mauve Austrian crystals. The brooch was owned by Dame Elizabeth Taylor in the 1960's. The brooch then became part of the collection of Carini D Auhesu, a collector of movie star memorabilia.

Elizabeth Taylor is pictured wearing a brooch very similar if not the same as she leaves a London hospital in 1961 after a severe bout of pneumonia.

Source: Rosyn Herman and Co of New York.

Still bearing the bandages from her tracheostomy operation, Elizabeth chats with several guests at the Coconut Grove Hotel, including Hollywood actor, Laurence Harvey, 1961.

Source: Douglas Kirkland/Corbis.

'I don't really know how to express my gratitude for this and for everything. I guess all I can say is thankyou, thank you from the bottom of my heart.'

- Elizabeth Taylor accepting her Oscar for Butterfield 8

The faux Ruby and Diamond earrings

The large teardrop shaped earrings have a silver plated metal base encrusted with dozens of glittering Austrian rhinestones. Although unmarked, professional appraisers attribute them as European, dating from the late 1950s. However, they are believed to have been purchased between 1960 -1970. It has been reported that the earrings were bought by Richard Burton for Elizabeth to wear as an accessory with her real ruby necklace. They both got a laugh from people complimenting her on the earrings, thinking they were real. At the charity auction, many items were offered and sold to numerous movie stars, museums, and personal collectors present that night. It is believed Dame Elizabeth personally attended the auction event, wearing the earrings on stage, and took them off and gave them to the highest bidder.

Source: personal psychic at the time, Michael J Kouri.

The faux Ruby and Diamond pendant necklace

This gorgeous teardrop shaped faux Diamond and Ruby pendant (Austrian Crystal rhinestones) was part of the original set owned and worn by Elizabeth Taylor at personal appearances, to parties and throughout her personal life, before she donated this piece to one of her AIDS charity benefits, where it was auctioned to the highest bidder. Dame Elizabeth received the original pendant and a nearly exactly matching pair of earrings made of real Diamonds and Rubies from Richard Burton. Through the years, when many female stars were being robbed, they had exact copies of their favourite pieces of jewellery made with high quality rhinestones from several well-known companies including Cartier, Eisenberg, and Weiss to name a few.

Source: personal psychic at the time, Michael J Kouri.

Seven months into the filming of *Cleopatra*, Elizabeth once again became seriously ill with a bout of Asian flu and could not work. Since her character was quite prominent in the movie, production was forced to shut down.

Doctors informed Elizabeth that the flu had now developed into a severe bout of pneumonia and that she would not survive should she remain in England.

On March 28, 1962, after 200 days of work, 20th Century Fox and producer Walter Wanger did not have a single foot of usable film to show for the millions of dollars already spent on the production of the film *Cleopatra* and moved the filming to Rome. Shooting began again in early August with a new director and screenplay, however not a new star.

Movie sets were rebuilt in Rome around the news that if Elizabeth stayed in London she would possibly die from pneumonia.

The Cleopatra costume

The costume budget for *Cleopatra* was $198,800.00. The costume count was 65 costumes. This costume was part of the collection. The jacket that accompanied it was worn in the final cut. This gown, however, was only worn during the screen testing. This gown was designed by Irene Sharaff and Vittoria Novaree who won "best costumes" and was to be worn with the burnt orange gown in the scene where Caesar dies in Cleopatra's arms. Unfortunately, it only made it the wardrobe rehearsals and not the final cut.

Like all Elizabeth Taylor costumes for the 1963 epic, *Cleopatra* they had to be taken in at the waist and out at the breast. This is full-length mustard yellow cotton blend gown. Embellished with serpent like embroidery up the left side. Gown is accompanied by a copy of the original sketch.

'Some of the Cleopatra costumes were fun--they even had real gold threads--and I wore them as evening dresses afterward!' -Elizabeth Taylor

The Victorian rocking chair

This rocking chair was housed in a trailer specially designed for Elizabeth Taylor during the filming of *Cleopatra* in 1963.

A late Victorian nursing rocking chair (smaller than average with no arms), carved walnut, upholstered in celery-green tufted velvet; owned and used by the star in her movie trailer on the set of many films for many years, in particular, *Cleopatra*.

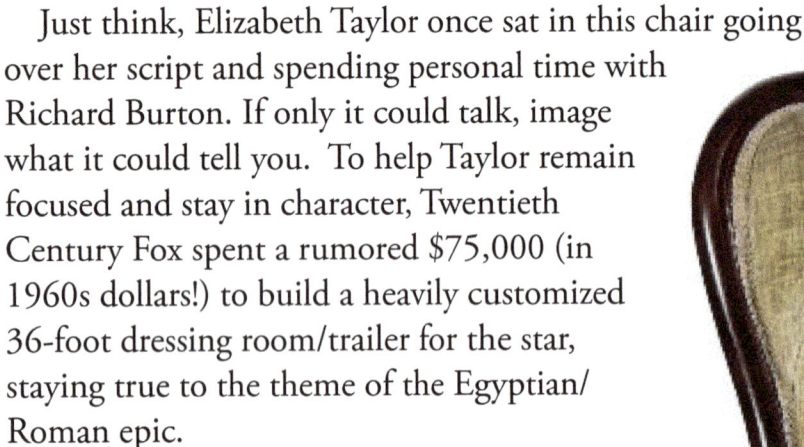

Just think, Elizabeth Taylor once sat in this chair going over her script and spending personal time with Richard Burton. If only it could talk, image what it could tell you. To help Taylor remain focused and stay in character, Twentieth Century Fox spent a rumored $75,000 (in 1960s dollars!) to build a heavily customized 36-foot dressing room/trailer for the star, staying true to the theme of the Egyptian/Roman epic.

The exquisite antique European rocking chair that Taylor sat in after filming every night was taken supposedly gifted to Michelle Breeze. Michelle worked as a double for Elizabeth Taylor on many of her movies including *The Sandpiper* (1965) and *Cleopatra* (1963).

Pictures are the original chair, top right, Michelle Breeze.

Source: United Press International, Heritage Auctions, and the Michelle Breeze estate.

Pictured is the original chair in Dame Elizabeth's movie trailer.

The Cleopatra movie props

This is a set of four Egyptian style props from the movie classic, *Cleopatra*, 1963. The items include:

- an Egyptian style tankard

- an Egyptian style date basket (five inches in diameter and 3 inches high)

- an Egyptian style faux opal jeweled and copper collar piece.

- The highlight is the faux lead knife, used during filming by Dame Elizabeth Taylor. The knife is inscribed E.T at the top of the blade. The handle is bound in soft leather and the blade has been tempered to resemble a knife that has born many a triumph. The majority of the film's props, including these four items, were custom made by Ellis Props, which only helped to increase the production's soaring budget.

Source: Ellis Props/ James McMahan.

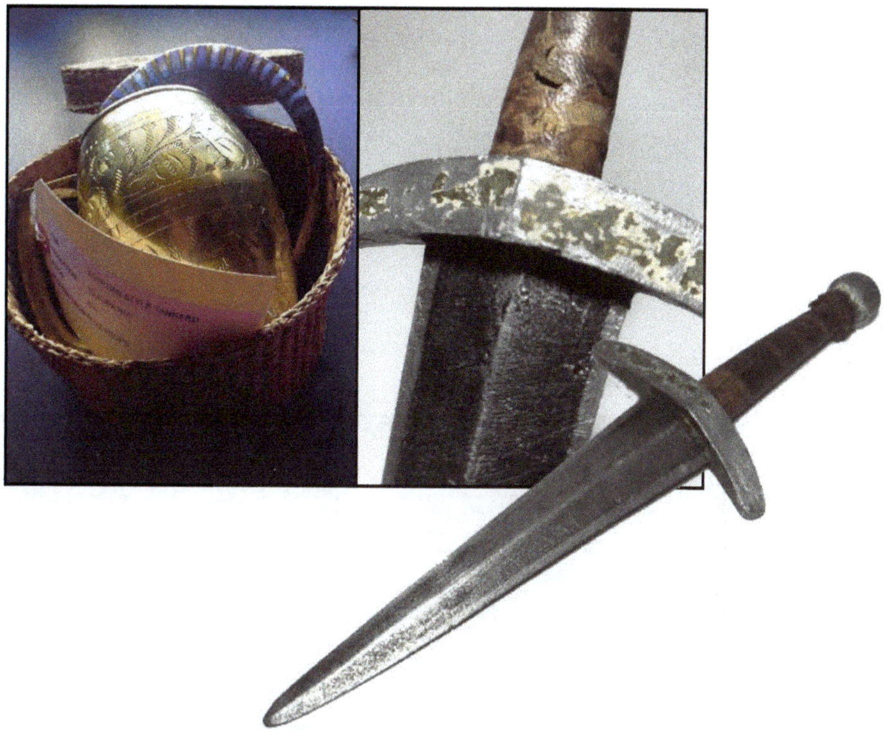

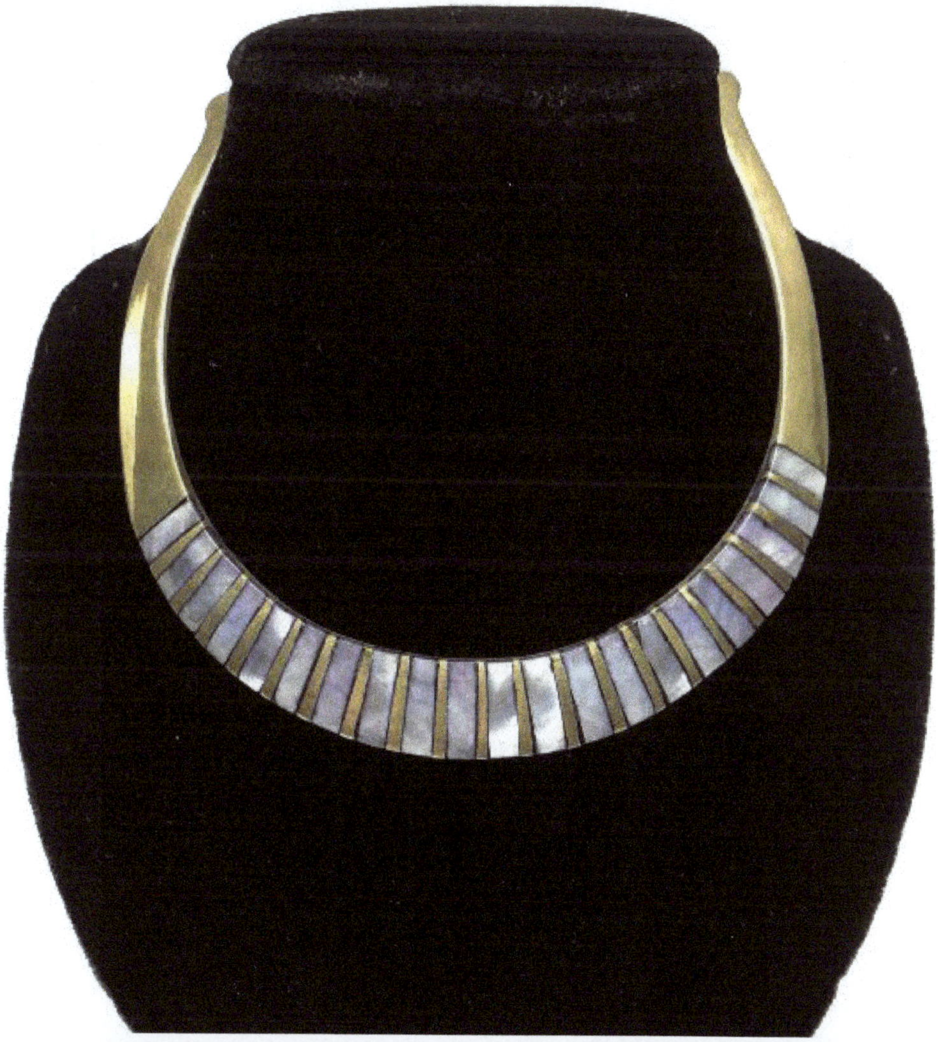

Elizabeth and Richards authentic autographs on the set of *Cleopatra*, 1963.

'I had first met Richard when I was 19, he flirted like mad with me and I thought, I'm not going to be another notch in your belt, Little did I know.'
- Elizabeth Taylor

'He had a wife at the time, she had a husband, they were madly in love.'
- Sydney Guilaroff, 1964

The lost paparazzi shots

At 10:30 am on December 9, 1963, Elizabeth relaxes in the backyard of 1315 Manzanta Avenue, Palm Springs, California.

Source: Gene Danieks/Black Star.

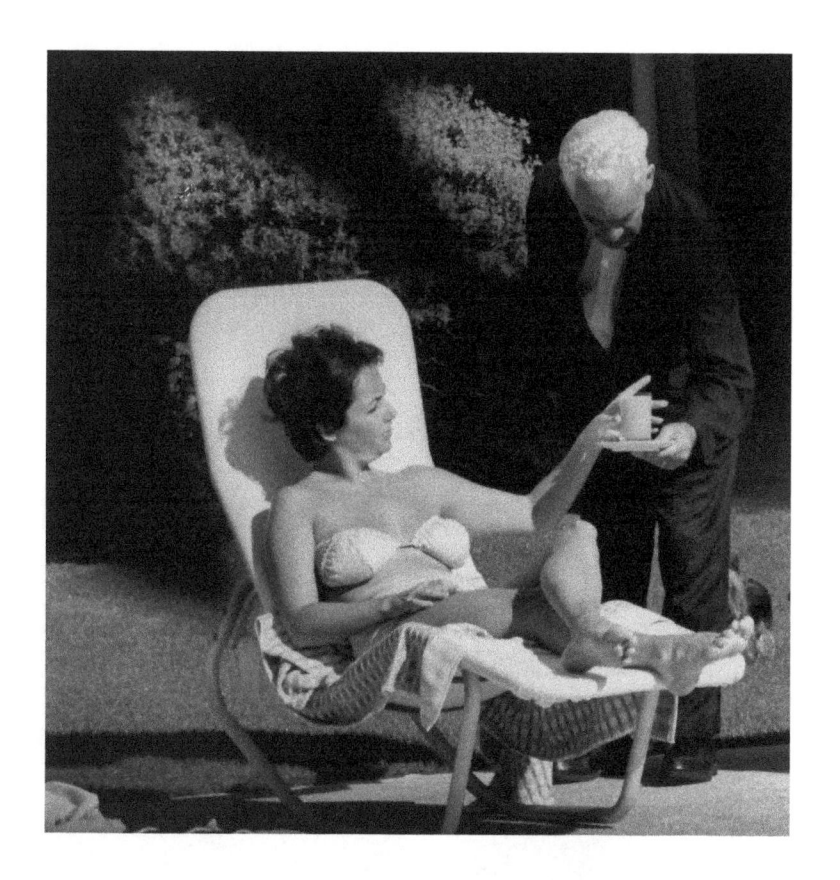

Elizabeth and Eddie Fisher are pictured here relaxing in the backyard of their rented house in Palm Springs and Elizabeth is served poolside by her butler.

The nineteen-sixties was the beginning of paparazzi photography. It would follow Elizabeth for the rest of her living days and claim her as one of the most photographed women in history.

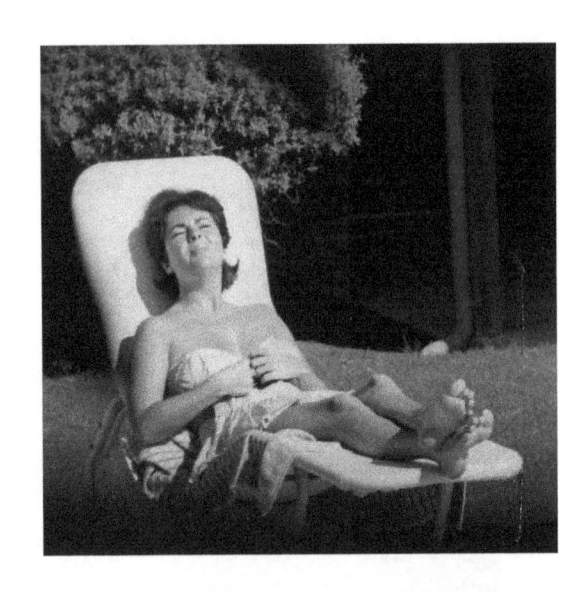

Elizabeth poolside, 1963

Source: Gene Daniels/Black Star.

The crepe hat

This is a dark blue crepe hat with pink flower accent. The hat was gifted from Dame Elizabeth Taylor to make-up artist to the stars, Ben Nye. It was then sourced from Star Past Inc film historians and memorabilia experts.

Hollywood make-up artist Ben Nye enhanced Elizabeth Taylor's beauty in *Cleopatra*.

Elizabeth Taylor is pictured getting off a boat wearing the same or similar crepe hat, whilst on holiday with then-husband, Eddie Fisher, 1964.

Source: From Ben Nye personal collection – Star past Inc. Film historians and memorabilia experts since 1987.

The cream woolen pants

A pair of cream woolen pants that were owned and worn by Dame Elizabeth Taylor and formed part of her wardrobe in the 1960's. Elizabeth is pictured here wearing similar if not the same trousers. They have been worn by Elizabeth and show wear on the inside lining.

Source: Julien's Auctions, California, USA.

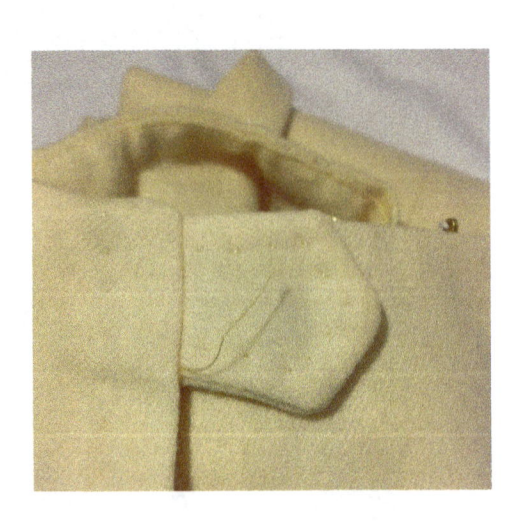

Mrs. Richard Burton

A romance that started in Rome, blossomed in London and bloomed in Mexico left Elizabeth with no other option but to divorce Eddie Fisher in Mexico and on March 6, 1964, dressed in a daffodil chiffon dress and with lilly of the valley flowers in her hair, Elizabeth said 'I do', for the fifth time. Hugging her new husband Mrs. Richard Burton said, 'Darling, I cannot believe it is really true that we are now husband and wife.'

Soon after the ceremony, Richard Burton returned to the set of *Hamlet*, in Toronto and on completion of the film joined his new wife in the MGM production of *The V.I.P's*, featuring Elizabeth as Frances Andros in an expensive furs and jewels made famous from the uniting of Taylor/Burton.

Elizabeth and Richard made eleven movies together, most of these were a reflection of their very own stormy, but passionate love life. It was often reported that 'Mr. and Mrs. Taylor' would often rent hotel suites above, beside and underneath them, so no one could hear the volatile arguing.

In 1964, the Burtons built a $200,000 house, equipped with swimming pool, high walls and fitted with burglar proof alarms, in the tiny village of Court Henry, Carmarthenshire, Wales.

' I'm so happy you won't believe it, this marriage will last forever.'

- Elizabeth Taylor

Mrs. Richard Burton

Dear Erica,

Thank you so much for your very kind letter.

I only wish it were possible for me to answer your request, but as I am sure you can understand, I receive hundreds of letters similar to yours and it would be impossible for me to select anyone as being more deserving. Therefore, I feel that I can best help by giving what I can to world-wide organizations, who in turn can help those who are in need.

I do hope you will understand and please accept our warmest good wishes,

Yours very truly,

Elizabeth Taylor Burton

The personal copy of National Velvet

Elizabeth Taylor was a special guest at a North American Riding for the Handicapped fundraiser in 1972. In attendance was Jane McClary. The film, *National Velvet* was played during the fundraiser and later gifted to Jane by Elizabeth Taylor.

Prior to this, the film had been sent to Mrs. Richard Burton care of Captain Pedro Claver of the Taylor/ Burton yacht "Katlizma", aptly named after their three daughters. This is the original case and movie reels that were originally sent to Dame Elizabeth Taylor from the MGM studios. It is therefore personally, addressed to Mrs. Richard Burton. The Film is 8mm television reels, used on a small projector but not in a movie theatre setting. The case is hard cardboard and is closed off with two canvas straps.

Elizabeth Taylor is pictured here with a lady with her back to the screen. This is Jane McClary circled in orange. The Taylor/ Burton motored yacht (KALIZMA) is also pictured was built in a London Pool in 1906 and weighs 276 tons.

Even during a press conference held at the Beverly Hills Wilshire Hotel, Elizabeth reflects a private feeling for her new husband Richard Burton, 1964.

Source: Gene Daniels/Black Star.

'I am so happy, you won't believe it, and this marriage will last forever.'

- Elizabeth Taylor

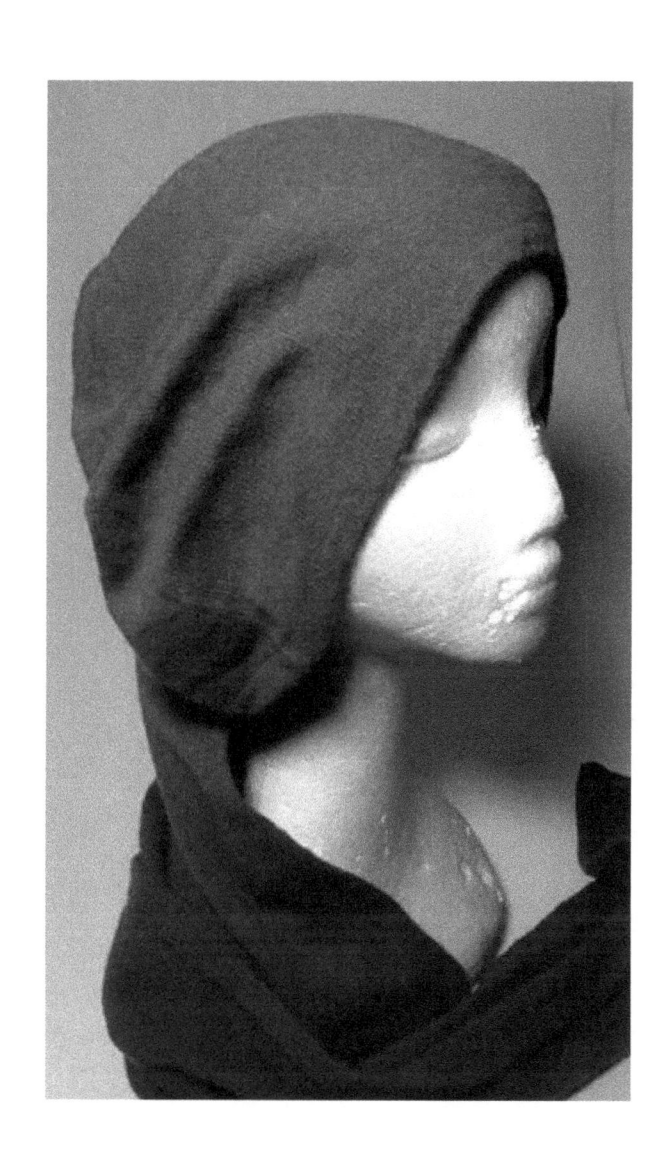

The Italian head wrap

This is a green woolen head wrap designed from "Next" Italy and once owned and worn by Dame Elizabeth Taylor. It was sold from collector to collector. Elizabeth Taylor is pictured wearing similar if not the same head wrap.

Source: From private collector to private collector.

'I miss you like something awful- for some reason especially today- so be all loving and tenderness tonight please and if you play your cards right I will take you out to dinner' – A love note from Elizabeth to Richard

Mrs. Burton's private jet

Mr. and Mrs. Burton make their way from the aircraft to the terminal where Richard is sorting out an issue with his passport, 1964.

Source: Gene Daniels/Black Star.

Elizabeth and Richard make their
way back to their aircraft, 1964.

Elizabeth and pooch Theresa, get ready to reboard their aircraft, 1964.

The correct way to enter your aircraft with
your loving pooch, by dearest Elizabeth 1964.

A secret look at the inside of the Taylor/Burton's private jet, 1964.

The jewelry case

This brown leather jewelry case circa 1965 has been specially monogrammed with the letter "E" for Elizabeth Taylor. The case measures 14 inches by 10 inches and contains several compartments and zipper pockets for the safe storage of jewelry.

Collector Barry Weiss was invited to Dame Elizabeth Taylor's estate after her passing and procured the leather case. He informed me that Elizabeth's people were most kind during the transaction. Unfortunately, he was required to sign a confidentiality contract and was unable to share any further information. The collection sourced the case directly from Mr. Weiss.

Barry first came to the public attention as the self-described "eccentric collector" in the reality television series "Storage Wars".

Source: Dales Madison Avenue New York/ Elizabeth Taylor's estate and Barry Weiss.

After the publication of her second book titled, *Elizabeth*, and the adoption of her fourth child, Marie Burton, Elizabeth was kept busy until her role in the 1965 film, *The Sandpiper*. This was Elizabeth's third movie directed by Vincente Minnelli and her paycheque for *The Sandpiper* was one million dollars. It was also another teaming up of Burton and Taylor that MGM hoped would prove a box office hit.

Prior to this, Elizabeth had ventured into television and did a show for the BBC, *Elizabeth in London*, for which she was paid $250, 000.

Source: Movie program, MGM/BBC.

MRS. RICHARD BURTON

Dear Evelyn

Just a note to thank you for your
kind letter telling me of your
enjoyment of both my husband and
me in our films. It was good of
you to take the time and trouble
to write and tell me.

With many thanks,

Yours truly,

Elizabeth Taylor Burton

Elizabeth replies to a fan (Evelyn) July 16, 1965.

The powder blue coat

This is a rare powder blue coat with three-quarter sleeves taken straight out of the closet from her Beverly Hills home. The label tells us that it is a "Ben Zuckerman of New York" fashion design, available only at the exclusive Beverly Hills luxury department store, I. Magnin.

This chain started in 1887, was eventually bought by Saks 5th Avenue and changed its name to Saks around 1994.)

Elizabeth Taylor is picture here in the coat, or if not, similar coat.

It was one of two outstanding coats sold at one of Julien's Auctions of Hollywood Celebrity Memorabilia in 2013. Labels read "Ben Zuckerman New York" and "I.Magnin." No size present. This powder blue three quarter sleeved coat was sold from Taylor's estate to the famous Julien's Celebrity Auction in Beverly Hills, in 2013.

It was then purchased by Michael and Fredericka Lam, the founders of The Great American Doll Company. In 2017, Michael Lam contacted the Elizabeth Taylor collection and sold this item to the collector in 2017.

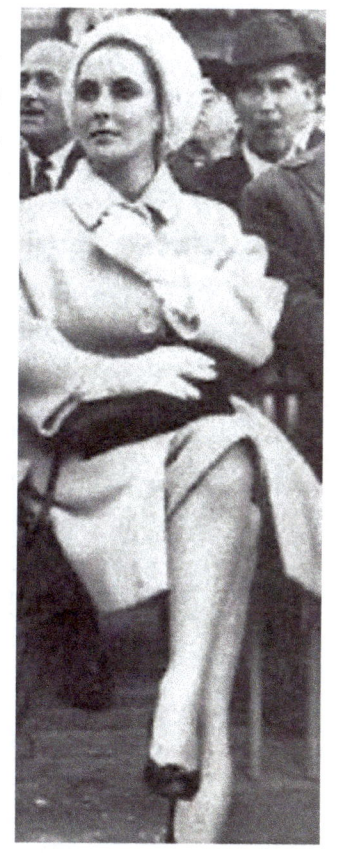

After winning a Golden Laurel Award for her role as Laura Reynolds in *The Sandpiper*.

Elizabeth teamed up again with her husband and gained 12 kilos to take on the role of, 'Martha' in the Warner Bros film, *Who's Afraid of Virginia Woolf?*. The Edward Albee screenplay was about a dysfunctional marriage and many times in the movie it was very hard to tell whether Richard and Elizabeth were actually in or out of character. Elizabeth took home $1,100,000 and 10% of the gross.

The Beverly Hills Hotel in Hollywood held the tenth annual Thailand Ball and with the help of the Burton's raised over $100,000 for the Thai Iain Clinic for Emotionally disturbed Children. Debbie Reynolds was chairperson of the board and Richard Burton was master of ceremonies

Elizabeth's father Francis was admitted to hospital after suffering a mild stroke. In New York, Tuesday, April 12, 1967, Elizabeth's portrayal as a drunken housewife in *Who's Afraid of Virginia Woolf?* won her second Academy Award. Neither Richard nor Elizabeth were present at the 39th Academy Awards ceremony as they were in France working on their Taylor/Burton production of their Royal Films International release of *The Taming of the Shrew*. As co-producers, Elizabeth and Richard earned 50% of the net profits made from the Columbia Picture release.

The drinking glass

This is a 1960s vintage drinking glass featuring an Egyptian theme. Egyptian figures, symbols, and cartouches are in white on an olive green background. The scene wraps around the entire glass. No maker's mark is on the bottom of the glass but it appears similar to glassware produced by Hazel Atlas.

The glass about 7 inches tall and in good condition overall with excellent colour.

The glass was used by Elizabeth to drink top shelf Courvoisier and Hennessey during film breaks on the set of *Who's Afraid of Virginia Woolf?*

The bar scene in *Who's Afraid of Virginia Woolf?* was filmed at the Red Basket Tavern in Southern Massachusetts. Elizabeth Taylor brought this glass along with her and used it off set between takes.

When filming at the Red Basket was complete, she left the glass behind - as a memento for the owner Lillian Glick or accidentally, Lillian was never sure.

The scene where Martha (Elizabeth Taylor) is speeding away from the Red Basket in her car had to be re-shot several times because Lillian Glick's dog got loose and chased the car. "CUT, will someone lock up that dog" she recalled.

Source: Lillian Gluck, owner and manager of the Red Basket Tavern, Southern Massachusetts in 1965.

The sterling silver money clip

A wonderful original Tiffany & Co sterling silver money clip, gifted to cameraman Alfred Daniel Baalas after the filming of, *Who's Afraid of Virginia Woolf*, in 1965. His initials "A.B." are on the back of the money clip. Alfred Daniel Baalas worked as an assistant cameraman for the Technicolor Picture Corporation, his wife as a film librarian. He worked for Mike Todd, Dame Elizabeth Taylor's third husband on, *Around the World in 80 Days* until Mike's death in a plane crash in 1958.

Elizabeth Taylor held an after-party at her Hollywood estate after the completion of *Who's Afraid of Virginia Woolf?* and invited the crew from the film. She presented the money clip to Alfred as a thank you. Alfred passed away on Feb 28, 2006.

Source: Alfred Daniel Baalas estate/ Victoria L Johnson, niece to Alfred Daniel Baalas.

One of Richard Burton's first jewelry purchases for Elizabeth was the platinum, mounted set with an emerald cut diamond weighing 33.19. It was often said that Burton's jewelry symbolised the strength of his love that he had for his wife. On May 16, 1968, Richard attended the Highly Important Jewels auction at the Parke-Bernet Galleries on Madison Avenue and placed a bid.

Richard Burton acquired the Krupp, a 33.19 carat Asscher cut Diamond for Elizabeth at the Park- Bernet Galleries in New York at the cost of $385,000. The Krupp diamond is regarded as one of the most flawless diamonds in the world. According to Elizabeth, 'the Krupp was her prize for beating Richard at ping-pong!' It was previously owned by Vera Krupp, who acquired it from Harry Winston jewellers.

The Krupp's had supplied the Nazi's with arms during the war, so, according to Elizabeth: 'When it came up for auction in the late 1960s, I thought how perfect it would be if a nice Jewish girl like me were to own it.' Burton won the ring in a bidding war that included Harry Winston. Since then the ring has rarely left Elizabeth's finger. The Elizabeth Taylor Diamond is a 33.19-carat (6.638 g) stone, formerly known as the Krupp Diamond, sold at Christie's on December 16, 2011, for $8,818,500.

The late nineteen sixties saw Elizabeth and Richard in many forgettable roles, including the Richard Burton directed film *Doctor Faustus*, the Warner Bros release of *Reflections in a Golden Eye*, in which Elizabeth played alongside Marlon Brando and the 1967 MGM film *The Comedians*, which critics claim was brought to a halt by the Burtons.

The Burtons appeared in another film, *Boom*, which co-starred Elizabeth's brother, Howard Taylor. It seemed that Elizabeth's movie star career had peaked and it would not be long before the flame between Richard and Elizabeth would start to flicker but it would never go out.

In the years' that followed, Elizabeth's father, Frances suffered another stroke in 1967 and died in 1968 aged 73.

Elizabeth's first husband, Conrad Nicky Hilton died on March 31, 1968, of a heart attack aged 42.

In 1971, *Zee and Co*, co-star Michael Caine begged Elizabeth to 'fluff' her lines as they filmed because she was outshining him with her performance. Michael Caine has since performed opposite a number of actresses in his career, including Nicole Kidman, Charlize Thereon and Scarlet Johansson, but insists that Elizabeth was the most impressive leading lady he had ever worked with.

'I remember I was doing a film with Elizabeth a long time ago and didn't know what to expect- lots of tantrums, probably. But she was completely professional, knew her lines before she turned up, never had a temper tantrum, she was quite amazing.' - Sir Michael Caine

The maxi dress

This is a 60s 70s vintage David Brown I Magnin California label loungewear hostess dress. A white and red dotted maxi dress. Dots are in varying sizes which were inspired by Op-Art, worn by the Oscar-winning actress, Dame Elizabeth Taylor.

Taylor was extremely well-known and liked both for her great acting accomplishments and for her charity activities which she pursued into her final days. This and other comfortable and loose-fitting elegant hostess gowns were often worn by her as she hosted many Hollywood parties and innumerable charity events. Julien's describes the gown as, "a graphic white floral print on a navy background, zip front, and matching belt." It has "David Brown" and Magnin labels, marked "Size M". Most of Elizabeth Taylor's David Brown hostess designs were purchased at this world-famous luxury Beverly Hills store, I. Magnin.

It just personifies her life and her style, even in her later years, and just creates its own subtle yet elegant ambience around it. We can only fantasize how she may have looked and felt wearing this as she casually mingled with her friends over cocktails and hors d'oeuvres at a mid-afternoon Beverly Hills pool party.

Source: Julien's Celebrity Auction in Beverly Hills/ Michael and Fredericka Lam, the founders of The Great American Doll Company.

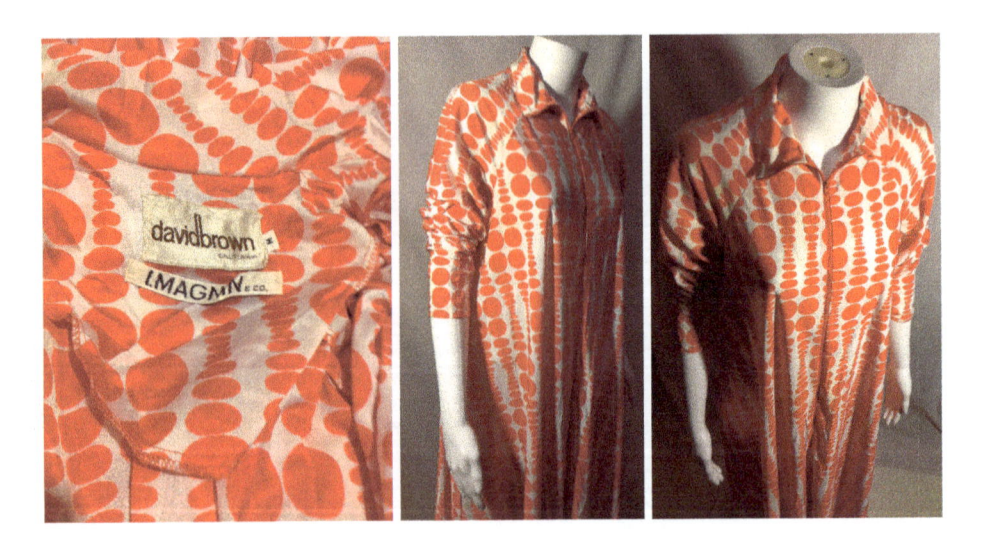

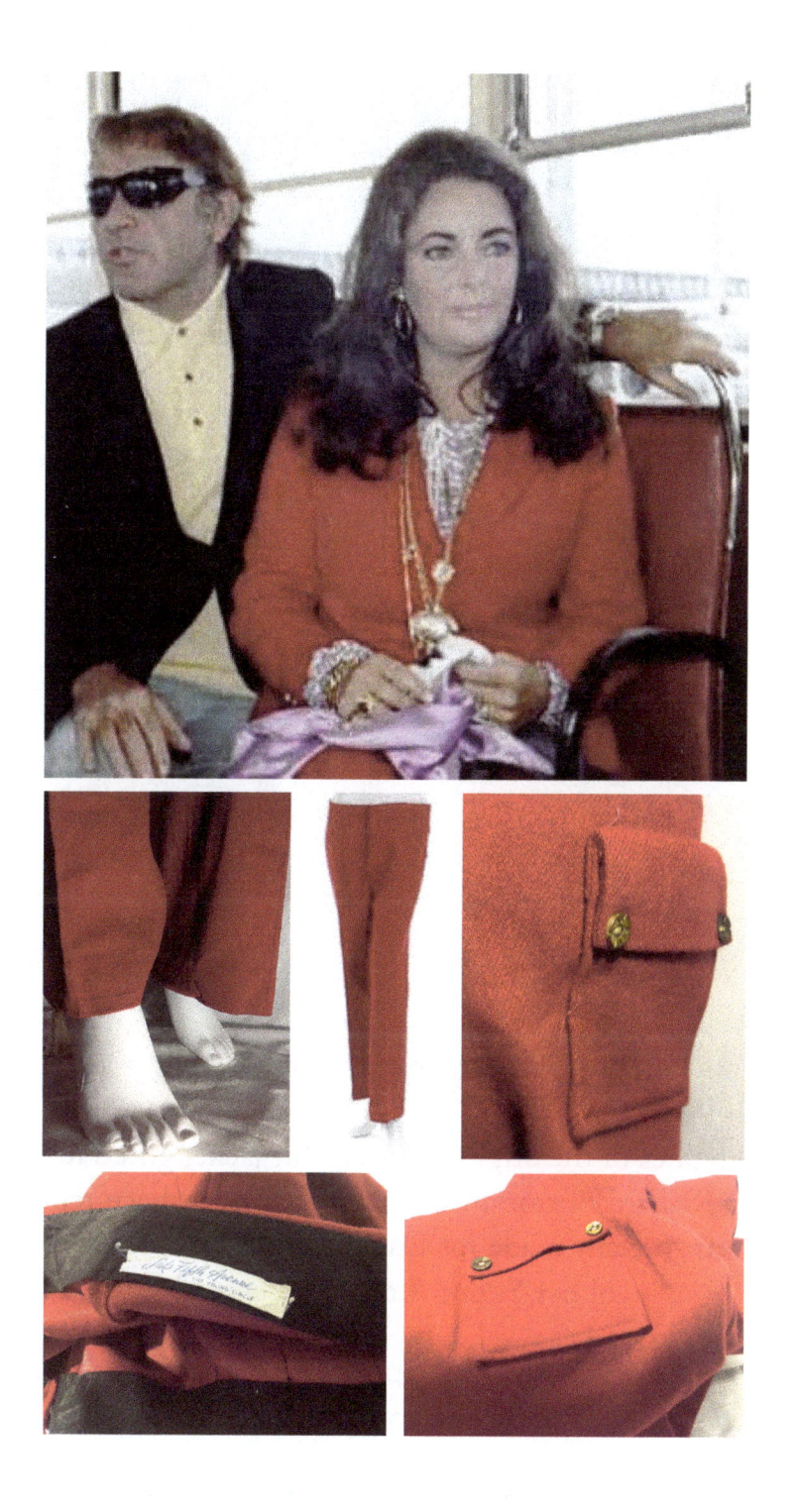

The red woolen pants

A pair of Elizabeth Taylor owned beautiful bright red wool trousers. This is a pair of bright red trousers labelled "Saks Fifth Avenue the Young Circle". No size present.

Sourse: Julien's Auctions in California /Jill's Treasures. Jill sold them onto the collection in 2017.

The Jaguar fur coat

This is a replica of the original leopard fur jacket gifted to Elizabeth Taylor by Richard Burton in June of 1963. It has been reported that the coat was specially made for Dame Elizabeth Taylor from the skins of five South American Leopards.

Source: Morocco, styled by Sportowne. Fabric by La France/ Wire Photo's 1968.

The costume brooch

This Nolan Miller faux sapphire and diamond flower pin is adorned with gold petals embellished with crystal rhinestones and is highlighted with a faux sapphire in the centre. Length is 2.5 inches and height is 1.75. Elizabeth Taylor is seen here in a scene from the 1972 film, *Under Milkwood* wearing a very similar item. This replica costume piece comes from the collection of fashion designer, Nolan Miller.

Source: Nolan Miller estate.

The director's chair

This director's chair was used by Elizabeth Taylor during the filming of *Hammersmith is out*, which co-starred then-husband Richard Burton.

The chair is a standard design but taller than average, wooden frame painted black, gray vinyl seat, backrest and attached script holder, small black plastic placard affixed to left arm reads "E.T.B." [Elizabeth Taylor Burton].

Elizabeth Taylor is pictured here sitting on a similar styled director's chair during her then-husband's filming of "Hamlet".

The film co-starred her husband, Richard Burton, in a re-telling of the Faust legend; interestingly, Taylor won a Silver Berlin Bear award for 'Best Actress' at the Berlin International Film Festival for this role of "Jimmie Jean Jackson".

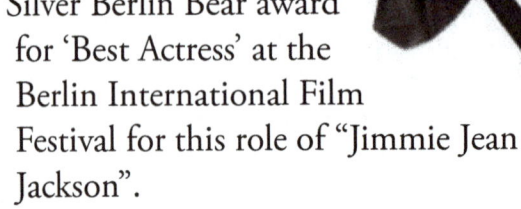

After production, she gift-wrapped the chair to her stand-in (double) and friend, Michelle Breeze, whose family later consigned it to this a Heritage Auction in 2017.

Source: Heritage Auctions, Texas/ Michelle Breeze estate.

Elizabeth Taylor is pictured here using the actual director's chair whilst taking a break on set with *Hammersmith is Out*, director, Peter Ustinov.

The bathing suit

This beautiful multi-coloured floral cotton blend bathing suit was owned and worn by Dame Elizabeth Taylor whilst on holidays with then-husband Richard Burton. Elizabeth Taylor is pictured wearing the bathing suit on the cover of Movie land 1973.

The suit is a one piece with sewn-in undergarment and fishbone bodice. This suit has no makers name or size; quite common as many celebrities and stars of the era did not want others to know their size or where they purchased their clothing.

Makeup artist to the stars Joseph King worked with Elizabeth Taylor on many films over her career. Elizabeth Taylor knew that Joseph collected items from his celebrity clients and gave him this item as a souvenir of their time together.

Source: Movie Land magazine/ Joseph King.

The lace skirt

This is a ten-tier cotton lined cream laced skirt that flows to the floor. The skirt was purchased by Dame Elizabeth Taylor during a holiday visit to Spain in the 1970's. It became a part of her personal wardrobe and was later gifted to J, Madeleine Munoz who was part of the Taylor staff for over 17 years.

Victorio & Lucchino is an Andalusian fashion firm , which takes its name from those of its creators, Victorio, José Víctor Rodríguez Caro, and Lucchino, José Luis Medina del Corral.

They began their journey in the world of fashion in the late 1970s , in the city of Seville.

At the beginning of the seventies, José Víctor Rodríguez Caro joined José Luis Medina (Lucchino) to present his own collections under the name of Victorio and Lucchino.

Source: Marina Del Rey California.

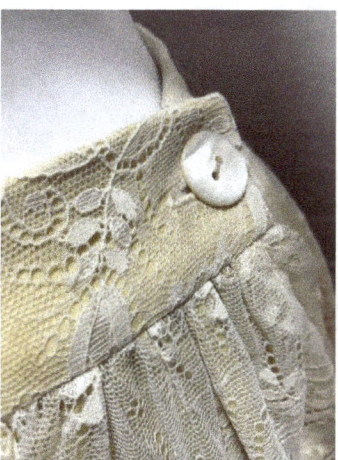

The plaid woolen pants

These plaid woolen pants labelled Saks Fifth Avenue, size ten came from the personal wardrobe of Elizabeth Taylor. Originally sourced by Julien's Auctions, California, from the home of Elizabeth Taylor. Elizabeth Taylor is pictured strolling the streets with her then-husband, Richard Burton, and wearing similar if not the same style trouser.

Source: Jill's Treasures. Jill's Treasures sells Celebrity owned item.

While Elizabeth and Richard's movie career may have been disappointing, their extravagant spending sprees gained them attention. Their new estate (Case Kimberly Estate) in Puerto, Vallarta, Mexico are two houses adjoined by a bridge. Elizabeth's house was on the left and meets her husband's on the right.

Elizabeth's private bathroom housed her favourite fragrance, Gardenia.

The Burton's teamed up for their very last film together *Divorce His, Divorce hers* in 1973. The ABC production portrays Elizabeth and Richard as a sophisticated couple, whose 18-year marriage is being split apart because of mutual indifference, quarrels, and adultery.

This was said to be close to the truth and on June 26, 1974, after a ten-year marriage, Elizabeth divorced her fifth husband.

Elizabeth made four films between 1973 and 1974. *Ash Wednesday*, *Night Watch*, *That's Entertainment and The Driver's Seat*. Critics slammed her performance as being a walk in the park. Her acting was not taken seriously and she was losing her radiance on the silver screen.

'I won't be a puppet anymore.'

- Elizabeth comments on her divorce from Richard Burton

The Casa Kimberly estate collection
The ashtray

This hand engraved sterling silver ashtray once belonged to Dame Elizabeth Taylor. Both Richard Burton and Elizabeth Taylor were heavy smokers during their time together. So much so that it is believed that Richard went and had an ashtray specially made for Elizabeth with her name engraved.

The ashtray is engraved "Elizabeth" in the style of Taylor's signature and believed to have been a birthday gift from husband, Richard Burton. The ashtray is stamped to verso: "Allan Adler Sterling". Interestingly, the design is based on a small tray in Adler's regular range, with two cigarette holders added on opposite corners.

Allan Adler was an American silversmith, known as "silversmith to the stars". Beginning his career as an apprentice in 1938, Adler designed silverware in shapes inspired by the Modernist art movement of the early 1900s. Other items he made included a silver belt for singer Michael Jackson and a silver lunchbox for Carol Channing, who carries the tin to banquets and awards shows.

Source: Julien's Auctions, USA/ Casa Kimberly Estate, Puerto Vallarta, Mexico.

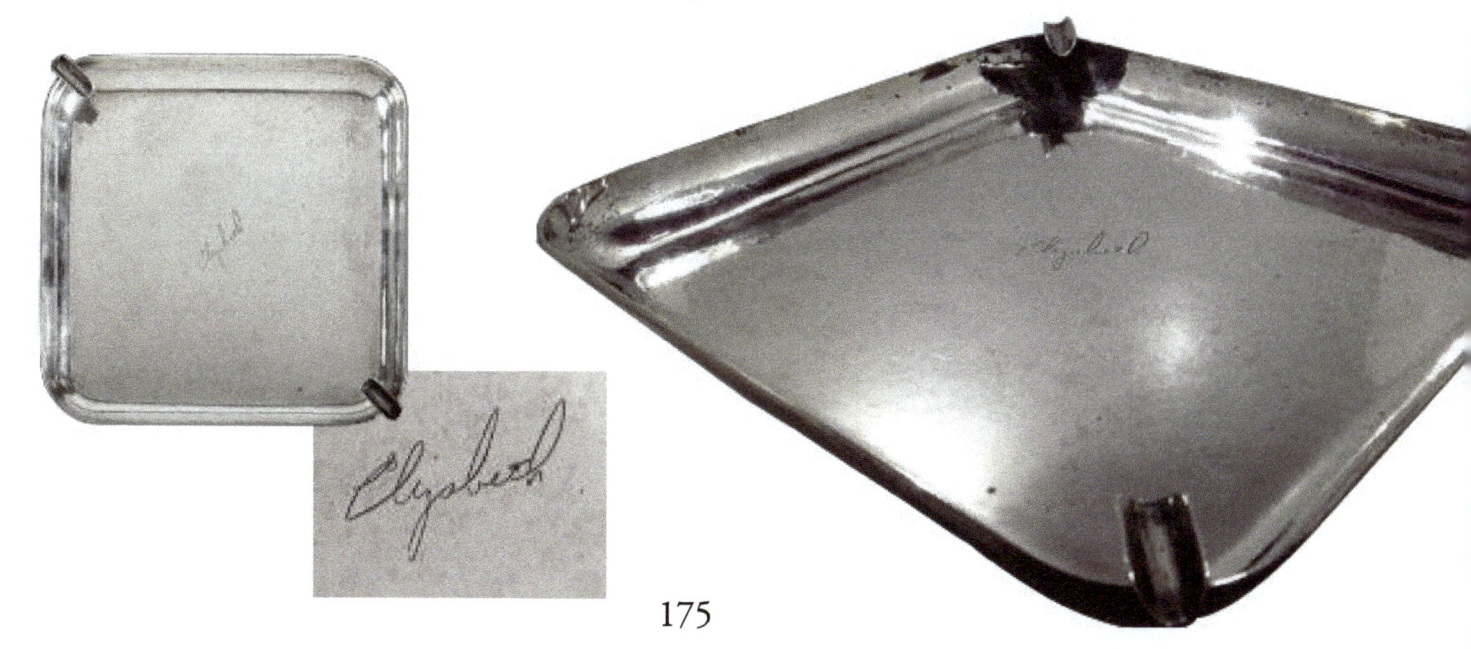

Collection of head scarves

These head scarfs were once part of Dame Elizabeth Taylor's personal Casa Kimberly wardrobe.

The first scarf is a psychedelic yellow floral patterned design on a white background. Each end of the scarf is embellished with white tassels it is made by Italian and Paris designers H.Bubois &CO.

The second is a multi- coloured dotted design including white, yellow, pink and orange dots on a pink background, which has no label.

Source: The personal wardrobe of Elizabeth Taylor, during her residence with Richard Burton at Casa Kimberly Estate, Puerto Vallarta, Mexico.1977. Christiana Auction Gallery NEWARK.

The maxi dress

This maxi dress is part of a collection of three worn by Elizabeth Taylor during her residence at Casa Kimberly, Mexico. This long sleeve maxi dress is printed with colourful psychedelic flowers and swirls. The cuffs are heavily embellished with large rhinestone, faux crystals, bugle beads, sequins, and palettes.

Source: The personal wardrobe of Elizabeth Taylor, during her residence with Richard Burton at Casa Kimberly Estate, Puerto Vallarta, Mexico. 1977.

The paper mache figurines

This is a set of two vintage Gemma Taccogna paper mache figurines. One represents a female form and the other a cat. Both figurines are designed to hold pencils. Both are hand-painted with bright colours and lacquered. These figurines once adorned the shelves of the Casa Kimberly home of Dame Elizabeth Taylor. Imagine the stories they could tell if only they could talk or even write with the pencils they carried.

Source: Gemma Taccogna paper mache figurines/ Casa Kimberly Estate, Puerto Vallarta, Mexico.1977.

The glass ice bucket

This beautiful clear glass container/ ice bucket with silver plated rim and lid measures 6' in circumference and is 7' tall. Elizabeth and Richard entertained guests on the veranda of their Casa Kimberly estate.

Elizabeth is pictured here on the Casa Kimberly veranda.

Source: Julien's Auctions California, Gene Daniels/Black Star.

The persimmon background

This is a sleeveless dress with a colourful ethnic print on a persimmon background. No size or label present.

Source: The personal wardrobe of Elizabeth Taylor, during her residence with Richard Burton at Casa Kimberly Estate, Puerto Vallarta, and Mexico.1977/ Julien's Auction House, Los Angeles.

The cotton shirt dress

This dress labelled, "By Nelly" is from a group of three worn by Elizabeth Taylor during her residence in Mexico. Elizabeth Taylor sold the home with some personal belongings in 1990. This powder blue cotton shirt dress is embroidered with bouquets of violets. When Elizabeth Taylor sold the house she left all her belongings, pictures and clothing there. She said it was too painful to be there after Richard Burton died.

Source: The personal wardrobe of Elizabeth Taylor, during her residence with Richard Burton at Casa Kimberly Estate, Puerto Vallarta, Mexico.1977/ Julien's Auction House, Los Angeles.

The blouse and trouser ensemble

This ensemble is from a group of three worn by Elizabeth Taylor during her residence in Mexico. Elizabeth Taylor sold the home with some personal belongings in 1990. Label reads "Luz originals".

Source: Elizabeth Taylor's personal wardrobe - Casa Kimberly Estate, Puerto Vallarta, Mexico. Julien's Auction House, Los Angeles.

The embroidered blouse

This is a white cotton blouse embroidered with orange and yellow flowers with faux ivory buttons.

Source: The personal wardrobe of Elizabeth Taylor, during her residence with Richard Burton at Casa Kimberly Estate, Puerto Vallarta, Mexico.1977/ Julien's Auction House, Los Angeles.

The lavender crystal perfume bottle

This is an authentic perfume bottle used and owned by Dame Elizabeth Taylor. Elizabeth Taylor gifted the bottle to Gordon Bau after the filming of *Who's Afraid of Virginia Woolf?* Robert Gordon Bau, known as Gordon Bau and sometimes as Gordy Bau (was head of the make-up department at Warner Brothers, 1930's to 70's. Gordon Bau was responsible for Elizabeth Taylor's make-up during filming in 1966. The bottle is made of crystal, clear lavender in colour and is a three-point shape. It stands five inches tall and comes with a crystal lavender stopper. It is said to have housed Dame Elizabeth's favorite fragrance, Gardenia.

Source: Gordon Bau Estate/ Roslyn Herman Antique and collectables.

The Alumesh handbag

Privately owned and used purse containing two movie ticket stubs that suggest Dame Elizabeth Taylor went to a movie using the purse. Price per movie ticket reads 20 cents. This Whiting and Davis alumesh off white handbag is inspired by the mesh pouch bag first designed by Paul Poiret in 1929.

Today Whiting and Davis still produce metal mesh in Massachusetts and have become renowned for their supply of mesh fabric for film garments and advertising campaigns.

Mr. Sydney Guilaroff was given the item as a memento after doing Elizabeth Taylor's hair for a premiere she attended in 1972.

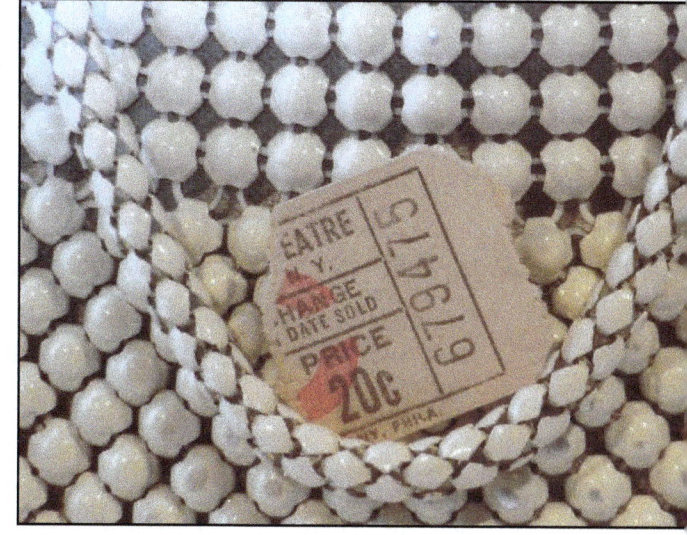

Source: Originated from estate of Sydney and Jose Guilaroff. Later John Le Bold and Film Historian and Memorabilia Expert acquired the item. It was sold to the collection in 2010.

Elizabeth made no movies in 1975, but she did briefly date Henry Weinberg and went on to remarry the love of her life Richard Burton. It seemed that she could not live with or without him. In fact, she actually loved him too much. They re-married again on October 10, 1975.

This was a reunion that lasted a mere eight months, as the couple could not reconcile their differences and divorced for the second time on July 26, 1976. Burnt out from her journey with Richard, Elizabeth entered into a romance with Senator John Warner which was considered a pleasing change of pace.

The public interest in Elizabeth was now focused on her increasing weight gain and not her professional profile. However, it seemed that time had not diminished her appeal and it would not be long before she found herself in the arms of her seventh husband.

At 44, Elizabeth married Senator John Warner on December 4, 1976, wearing a knee-length cashmere dress, tweed coat with trimmed grey fur and carrying a bouquet of wild heather.

In 1976, Elizabeth joined Edward Lewis and director George Cukor in the film *The Blue Bird*, which became the very first Soviet- American co-production in film history and the most expensive musical ever made.

This is an original signature from Elizabeth who played three characters in the film, *The Blue Bird*, 1976.

Source: Len Film Organisation.

Head scarf

The scarf is a yellow and black scarf made by H. Dubais and Co. It is a black and daffodil yellow plaid scarf with hand rolled edges with a label that reads, "Handwoven in France for H. Dubais and Co, Paris. Elizabeth Taylor is pictured here cooking her favorite southern fried chicken at Atoka farm, Middleburg, Virginia, 1977 in a similar if not the same scarf.

Source: Julien's Auction House, Los Angeles.

Please credit: FirooZ Zahedi

The Valentino pant suit

This is a Valentino two-piece tan cotton blend vest and pant suite. Comprising of a button-down vest with envelope pockets and matching trousers. Label reads, "Valentino". Elizabeth Taylor is pictured wearing the outfit as she attends a costume fitting for the movie *The Blue Bird* at the Ritz Hotel in Paris1976. Some years later Princess Diana would be captured on CCTV leaving the Ritz Hotel in Paris shortly before her death in a car crash in 1997.

From the auction of the collection of Elizabeth Taylor held to raise funds for the Elizabeth Taylor Aids Foundation after her passing in 2011.

Source: Christies Auction House Los Angeles.

Elizabeth was once again immortalised in the doll form, which resembled more of her home life seen on the farm with John Warner, than on the silver screen.

Source: Horsham/Len Film Organisation.

The Valentino green turtle neck

Elizabeth is seen here, wearing the turtle neck with new husband, John Warner.

This dark green Valentino turtle neck sweater comes from the wardrobe of movie legend Elizabeth Taylor, 1979.

Source: Disneyland Attractions/Peter Boulin.

In 1978, Elizabeth appeared in yet another movie musical, the Harold Prince production of, *A Little Night Music*. For the very first time Elizabeth was required to sing, really sing. She sung, Send in the Clowns.

By 1979, Elizabeth had announced that she was putting the Taylor- Burton diamond up for sale and planned to use part of the proceeds to build a children's hospital in Botswana. In June of that year Henry Lambert, a New York Jeweller bought the diamond for a staggering $5,000,000.

'Thirteen stone, that's a boiling piece that came with many unkind jokes.' 'The one I heard most, Elizabeth was seen in town today wearing a yellow dress, and school children were running to the bus to board her.'

- Elizabeth Taylor

'I wanted to grow old with somebody, on the farm, in front of the fire place and read books.'

- Elizabeth Taylor

The Taylor/Burton diamond is sold to raise funds to
bulid a childrens' hospital, 1979.

The chiffon evening gown

This is an authentic beautiful full-length pink chiffon layered gown. It appears to have been custom made, as it is unlabeled and no size is evident. Dame Elizabeth Taylor appears in a gown similar if not the same with then-husband John Warner, on the cover of People Magazine 20 October 1980.

The gown was given to Sydney Guilaroff, who worked with Elizabeth Taylor on many of her films, including, *The Blue Bird, Who's Afraid of Virginia Woolf?* and *The Sandpiper* among a few.

Source: Sydney Guilaroff estate 1988.

John Warners autograph, 1979.

An original Elizabeth Taylor Warner autograph, 1979.

Source: Italy.

The butterfly and circle dress

This is a short-sleeved A-line dress. It ties at the front and is printed with large butterflies and circles on an emerald and white background. Label reads "Frankie Welch". Designed by Frankie Welch who is a designer best known for printed scarves and designing the gown Betty Ford wore to her husband's presidential inauguration. A sketch by unknown designer captures Elizabeth Taylor Warner's fashion sense at the time. Elizabeth is also pictured wearing a similar design.

Source: Julien's Auction House, Los Angeles.

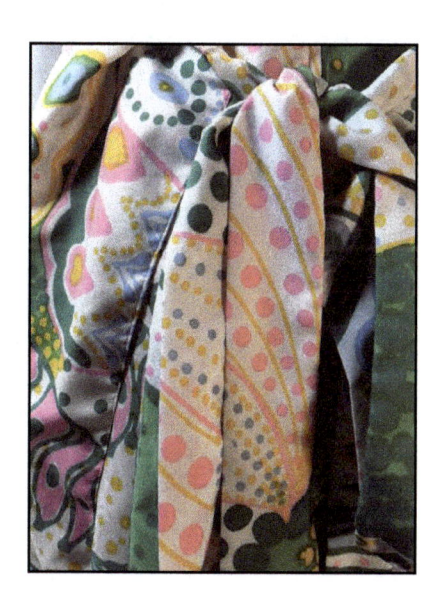

Just several weeks after they are married, Mr. and Mrs. Warner take a drive down a street in Manhattan during the time of her Broadway appearance in *Little Foxes*, November 1981.

Source: Bob Scott.

In 1981, Elizabeth still a senator's wife, took to the stage in Zev Buffmans production of *The Little Foxes*. It seemed that it was Broadway and not Washington that gave Elizabeth a real, new direction in her mid-life. While making her Broadway and West End debuts in the 1982 revival of the Lillian Hellman's *The Little Foxes*, she was at the same time in preproduction of Noel Coward's *Private Lives* in which she has reunited yet again with the love of her life, Richard Burton.

After the season run of, *The Little Foxes*, Elizabeth returned to her simple life on the farm. Becoming more and more overwhelmed by her personal failure, she knew in her heart that she had become an emotional mess. So much so she even gave herself her own nickname, 'boiling piece.'

Elizabeth was physically and emotionally exhausted by chronic health problems, public responsibilities and gruelling schedules had once again taken their toll on Elizabeth's movie star brilliance.

Longing to return to what she knew best, Elizabeth purchased Frank Sinatra's old house at 700 Nimes Road, Belair, California for two million dollars on February 2, 1982. This address would be my primary contact with Elizabeth and she lived there until her passing in 2011.

Elizabeth called it a day and divorced John Warner on November 7, 1982.

'I knew that I was plunging and the ultimate result would be death, so I had to do something dramatic to pull myself out.' 'I was drinking so much, so I thought what would be the most challenging thing to do?'

'When politics came along, John was married to the senate, I couldn't cope with that.'

- Elizabeth Taylor

The pillbox

This is a beautiful genuine "Pill Box" decorated with the image of a young blonde girl. Image unknown. It is a heart-shaped object made from tin with a hard plastic insert. This is a rare find or keepsake. Global Antiques has made every effort to verify the existence and providence of this item. Unfortunately, no additional information was provided regarding this item. It was purchased directly from Global Antiques under strict privacy agreements. Greg Jones is the "curator" of Global Antiques and authenticator and consignor of such Historic Souvenir.

Source: Los Angeles Global Antiques.

Elizabeth holds a press conference during her West End debut in *The Little Foxes*, 1982.

Elizabeth declines a party invitation

This an extremely rare handwritten short letter or note undated but is circa 1982-1983 when Taylor began staging a comeback to show business with appearances on Broadway in *Little Foxes* and on TV's *General Hospital*.

In the letter, she declines a party invitation and uses very colourful language, describing her weight - around the period where she had noticeably gained weight - as "f'...d up" and also cursing an inoperative answering machine!

She signs her signature as "Elizabeth Taylor Warner," reflecting her then marriage to U.S. Senator John Warner of Virginia, also helping pin down the timeline to the early 1980s. The stationery letterhead also reads the same.

This is a unique piece of personal memorabilia from Elizabeth in her own hand and referencing what was tabloid fodder at the time before she staged a triumphant return to the glamour that had defined her earlier career.

The vintage faux ruby bracelet

Elizabeth Taylor gifted this stage-worn piece of jewelry to Matilda Kupp after the Broadway run of *Little Foxes*. This vintage costume ruby bracelet is a production piece worn by Elizabeth Taylor during the stage show, *Little Foxes*. She is pictured wearing it during the Broadway run.

Matilda Kupp assisted Elizabeth Taylor during numerous productions and became a good friend with her over the years. Elizabeth gifted many personal items during her 70-year career, as tokens of her appreciation.

Source: Matilda Kupp Estate. Sold to this collection by Dave W. Kupp, executor of the estate.

Celebrating her 52nd birthday Elizabeth was turning to drugs and alcohol for the relief of her pain and inner emotional turmoil. On December 5, 1983, Elizabeth became the very first star to enter the Betty Ford Centre for alcohol and drug dependency treatment.

She was released from the Betty Ford Centre on December 20, 1983, still suffering severe back pains. Continued health problems would see Elizabeth spend many of her later days confined to a wheelchair and her roller coaster ride with weight and drug dependency would be played out many times over her legendary life.

The adoring public knew that their very own queen of Hollywood was suffering from grief and depression. Food and drink were said to be her only comfort in her darkest hours.

'I am so glad that I asked for help, I was stuttering, stumbling, and incoherent. I had used sleeping pills for over 25 years I learned to rely on them.'

-Elizabeth Taylor

The waist length jacket

This is an authentic purple wool waist length jacket with a fur collar. It is embellished with two detailed buttons. The item has no labels or size and has been custom made. It is a jacket that was worn by Dame Elizabeth Taylor to a special occasion in 1983. An item originally gifted from Dame Elizabeth to the hairdresser of the star Sydney Guilaroff who worked with Elizabeth Taylor on many of her films.

Source: Sydney Guilaroff estate 1995.

Elizabeth and Richard arrived for the final night of *The Private Lives*, 1983.

Source: Walter Miller Jnr.

'He will never ever leave me, in a way I don't think that our relationship will ever end.' 'Two months before Richard died he said to his brother, oh that bloody women, I still love her, and I know one day I'm going to end up marrying her again, even if it's in heaven.' 'We couldn't stay away from each other.'

- Elizabeth Taylor

The black leather bootss

This is a pair of beautiful black soft leather boots with three-inch heels used and worn by Dame Elizabeth Taylor to the Los Angeles airport in the late 1980's.

Source: Richard Wilson.

Original photograph of Elizabeth and Burt Reynolds was taken by Roddy McDowall at Rock Hudson's Californian estate in 1983.

Source: Rock Hudson Estate/Martin Flaherty.

Elizabeth and good friend Liza Minnelli pictured here, backstage at an AIDS fundraiser May 5, 1983.

Elizabeth made a brief come back on the small screen in 1984 made for television movie *Between Friends*, by Lou Antonio and also made a cameo appearance in Vince McEveeties, *Hotel*. On August 5 the same year, the man she loved so much, passed away in Switzerland. Richard Burton was 59. Elizabeth was devastated at the loss of the man she loved so much that she had married him twice.

Several months later Elizabeth received more devastating news, after becoming ill earlier in the year, her former co-star from the 1956 film *Giant*, Rock Hudson, died October 2, 1985, of an AIDS-related illness, he was 60.

Elizabeth's love for the silver screen had now been replaced with her passion for human rights and her love for men had been conquered by the need to embrace those in need of human compassion. In supporting AIDS charities, Elizabeth took up a cause that was often frowned upon by her colleagues and friends.

The Laura Biagiotti sunglasses

This is a purple/blue clear pair of sunglasses designed by Laura Biagiotti.

They were owned and worn by Dame Elizabeth Taylor, (Pictured) most memorably when she tried to visit the gravesite of her fifth husband Richard Burton in Celigny, Switzerland, 1984. Some years later in 1988, Dame Elizabeth is pictured wearing the same glasses as she leaves the LA hospital in a wheelchair.

Elizabeth Taylor donated the glasses to a Celebrity Wares store to help raise money for a local animal shelter. They were bought from the store by a collector and later sold to the collection.

Source: Star Wares on Main, Santa Monica.CA.

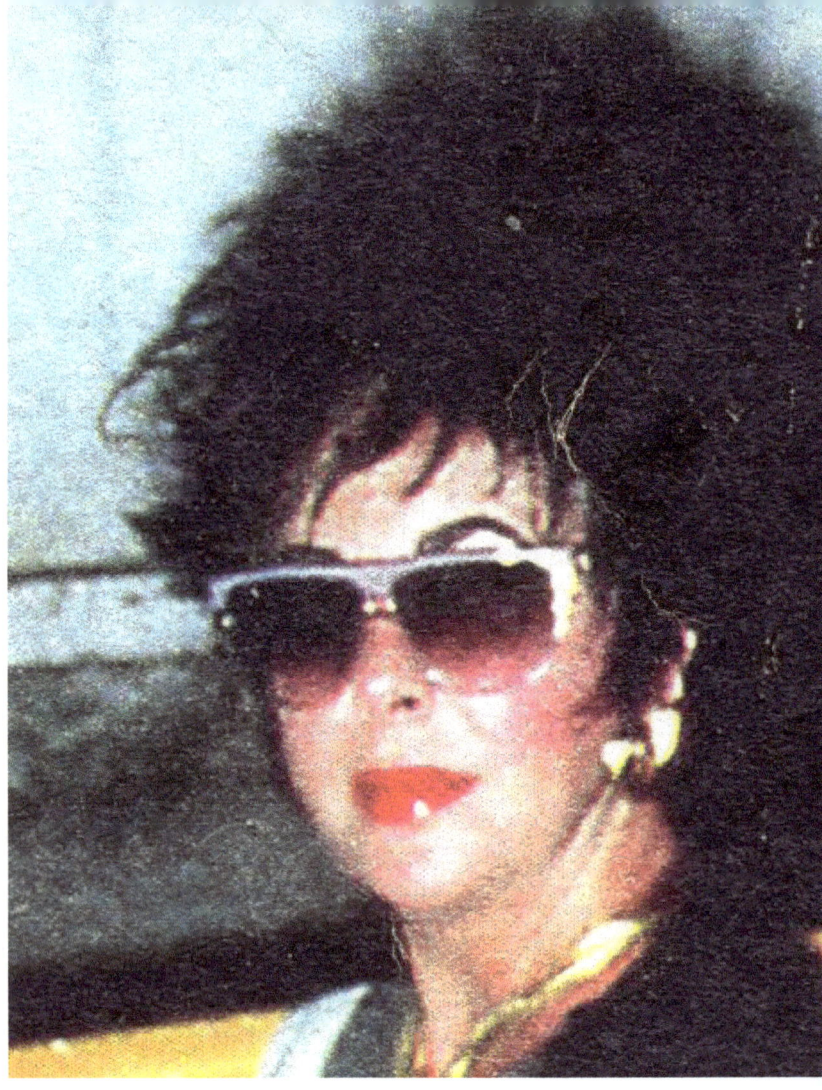

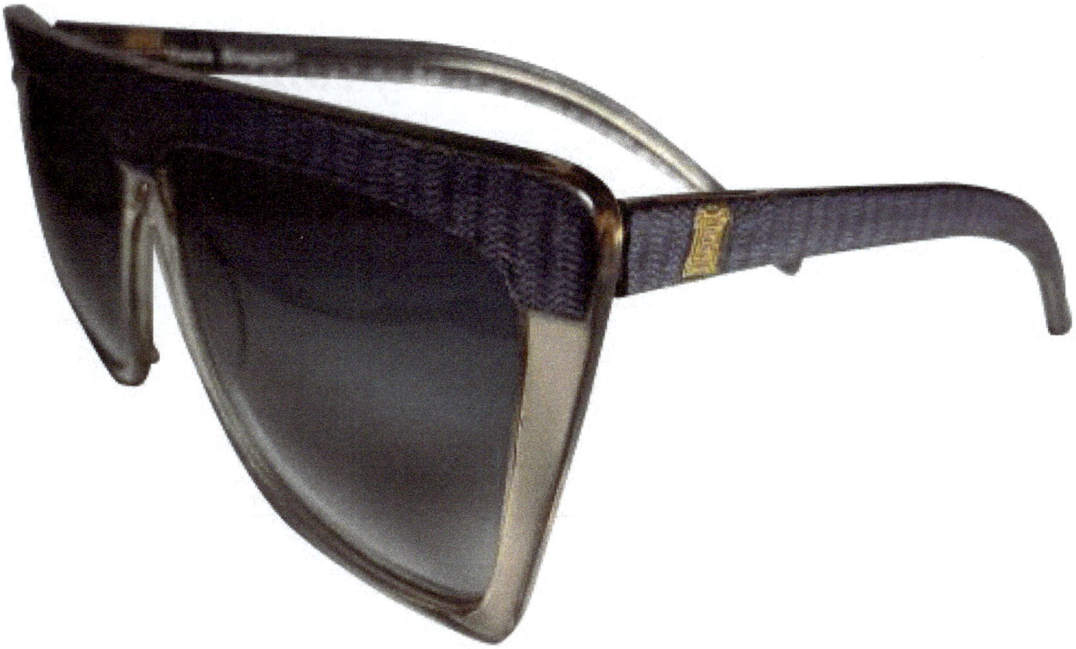

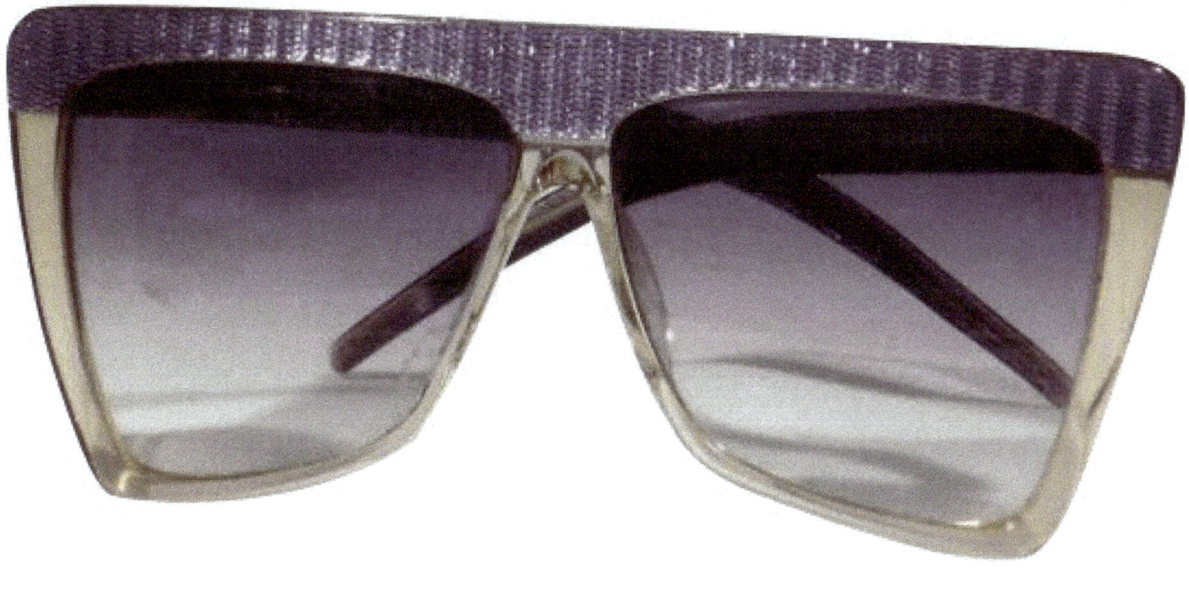

Elizabeth's letter of condolence

Ross Hunter, Oscar-nominated Hollywood producer writes to Dame Elizabeth two weeks after the loss of her friend and co-star Rock Hudson. Ross had teamed Rock Hudson up with Doris Day in the romantic comedy, "Pillow Talk", 1959.

Pictured is an extract from the original letter from Ross to Elizabeth Taylor.

> It's tough to face the fact that Rock is no more.
> I pray the circus atmosphere that surrounded him during his last months will be forgotten and that he'll be remembered by the public as the darn good actor he was. Those he chose as friends, know what a darn good friend he was.
> Jacque sends love,
> As does,
> Ross

The cashmere blanket

This item was given to Joan Collins from Dame Elizabeth Taylor when Joan Collins married Peter Holm on 3 November 1985. He became her manager and co-produced two of her television mini-series with her, Sins and Monte Carlo. Collins kept it in her personal storage unit in Van Nuys, California.

She later consigned it from JM Media Group to Star Wares Celebrity store. It was purchased from the store for this collection.

Source: JM Media Group/ Star Wares Celebrity store.

Elizabeth and Carol Burnett appear here in the television movie, *Between Friends*, 1985.

Good friends Bob Hope, Shirley MacLaine and Elizabeth, 1985.

Source: Yani Begakis.

'Rock Hudson's death activated Elizabeth into some kind of movement.'

- Shirley MacLaine

Dame Elizabeth took to the stage at the Golden Globe Awards, to receive yet another accolade, the Cecil B De Mille Award, 1985.

Source: Bob Scott.

It appeared that public opinion had preserved the celebrity of Elizabeth and the public's fascination never faded. Elizabeth received two other awards in 1985, The Golden Apple award (female star of the year) and the Women in Film Crystal Award.

Since her very first Golden Globe in 1957, Elizabeth had received over 30 awards for her work on the silver screen and so importantly for the work that she embarked in the nineteen eighties, namely her AIDS charities and her passion for human equality.

Elizabeth was no longer the Hollywood screen goddess of the sixties, she had now transformed into an activist, using her celebrity to speak up against the immorality of modern society. Elizabeth used her celebrity to raise awareness and bring financial gain to a topic that would later become her life's work. She soon left her Hollywood persona behind and became an outspoken warrior in the daunting battle against AIDS.

In 1985, her fees to appear in the television movies, *Malice in Wonderland* and the television miniseries co-starring Patrick Swayze in *North and South* raised over 200,000 dollars for her insatiably loved AIDS charity.

The North and South velvet gown

In the mid-nineteen-eighties Elizabeth wore a lot of Hollywood designer Nolan Miller costumes and clothing. He was also famous for the outrageous costumes in the nineteen-eighties TV drama, *Dynasty*. In her role as Madame Conti in the TV series, *North and South*, Elizabeth wore this black velvet gown.

Source: Nolan Miller/Heritage Auction House Texas.

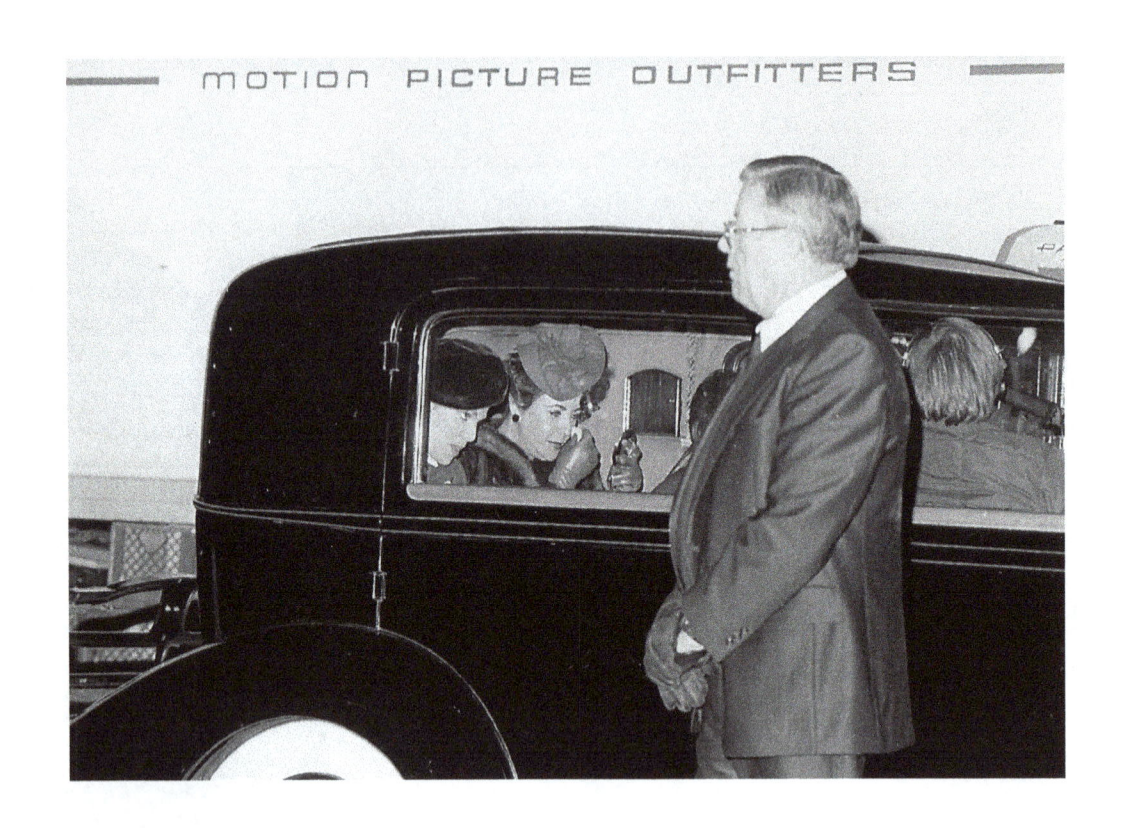

Elizabeth does her own makeup on the set of *Malice in Wonderland*, 1985.

'I went to a hospice outside of Rome, it was all AIDS patients and the society ladies of Rome couldn't walk their dogs near this building, because they thought AIDS was an airborne illness and that their dogs might catch it.'

'The ignorance.'

'I went inside and said Is there anything we can do for you? One man said, To have someone put their arms around us. I still feel the stinking of tears in my eyes, as I kissed each and every one of them.'

-Elizabeth Taylor

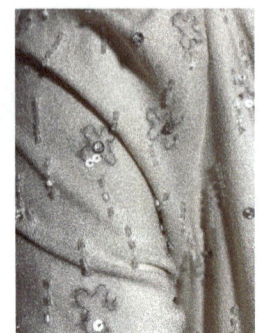

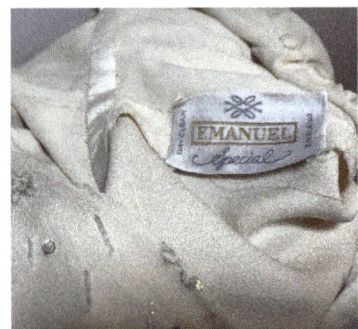

The evening dress

This is an item donated by Dame Elizabeth Taylor to a celebrity store to raise money for a local animal refuge. This evening gown is an off-white crepe style embellished with clear beads throughout. It ties at the waist with a flowing bow. It was created by British designers Elizabeth Florence Emanuel and her former husband David Emanuel, best known for their 1981 work for the wedding of Diana, Princess of Wales.

The gown was designed for Elizabeth Taylor to attend the 1985 Oscar ceremony, where she was accompanied by George Hamilton.

Source: Arlyn Rudolph of Celebrity Seconds, Palm Springs, CA. USA sourced this item from the personal wardrobe of Elizabeth Taylor. The item was then sourced for this collection from the Celebrity Seconds store, which has now closed after Elizabeth Rudolph passed away in 2014.

The Oscar Gown

When attending the 1986 Oscar ceremony Dame Elizabeth Taylor emerged looking as stunning as ever in this specially designed Nolan Miller gown. The corsage formed bodice is highlighted with a shirred bust line gigot style, three quarter length sleeves. The waist and cuffs are finished with a point, the back of the skirt features a sunburst pleat between full-length ruffles, adorned with pink silk stemmed roses.

Source: Christies Auctions/ Nolan Miller estate.

The sequined evening gown

This sequined long flowing evening gown was designed for Dame Elizabeth Taylor by Hollywood designer, Nolan Miller, to wear to the 1986 Oscar Ceremony. She, however, chose another of his designs instead. This Nolan Miller sequined gown has a blouse draped bodice and spaghetti straps that flow to a floor-length flared skirt forming a train.

The gown is of an abstract netting in lavender, gold, and silver embroidered with gold thread in a meandering line, embellished with sequins in silver and lavender over a lavender crepe lining. The side zipper closure exposes the Nolan Miller label to the rear. Included is the original marker and glitter sketch for the gown, signed by Nolan Miller and labelled Elizabeth Taylor.

Source: Heritage Auction House, Dallas, Texas/ Nolan Miller estate.

Placid Domingo and Elizabeth at the Franco Feffirelli premiere of Turandot, March 12, 1987. Elizabeth would later appear in Zeffirelli's, *Young Toscanini*.

Source: Harmonie Autographs and Music INC.

In 1987, Elizabeth launched her very first perfume titled *Passion*. It became the biggest grossing celebrity perfume of all time and earned Elizabeth over $70,000,000 in its first year. Today it still earns the Taylor estate in excess of 3.3 million dollars a year.

Earlier that year Elizabeth's love interests included billionaire magazine tycoon, Malcolm Forbes, and the handsome George Hamilton. Looking the most glamorous she had in several years, Elizabeth made a small screen comeback in the 1987 movie *Poker Alice*, which was met with positive reviews by the critics. Elizabeth still had movie star allure.

At 55 years of age, Elizabeth was now the founder and chairperson for the American Foundation for AIDS Research (Am FAR) with co-founder Mathilde Krim and every dollar raised since 1985, has gone to provide services to AIDS victims and give preventative information to the public, worldwide.

Dame Elizabeth Taylor promotes her new fragrance, *Passion* at Macy's Sanfrancisco West, October 15, 1987.

ELIZABETH TAYLOR'S
PASSION

October 5, 1987

Dear "Passion" Customer,

Congratulations on your "Elizabeth Taylor's Passion" purchase from Macy's.

I am very pleased that you'll be joining Macy's October 15 for tea with Ms. Taylor.

We will begin seating for the tea at 3:45 p.m. The tea will be held on the 8th floor of Macy's San Francisco West. Please take the elevator to the 8th floor where you will be greeted by our host or hostess.

We ask that you bring this letter and present positive photo identification of yourself. Of course, the invitation is non-transferable. Cameras and recording devices are prohibited.

We are very excited to welcome Elizabeth Taylor to San Francisco and look forward to seeing you on October 15.

Warmest regards,

Elizabeth M. Krogh

Elizabeth Krogh
Vice President, Public Relations
and Special Events

Please R.S.V.P. to: Macy's Special Events
at (415) 393-3889.

macy's

Elizabeth was looking the most glamorous she had in several years playing Alice Moffat in the 1987 television movie, *Poker Alice*. Elizabeth, after all these years had the luring power of a true movie star. Hollywood costume designer, Nolan Miller was appointed to do all the costumes for the film.

For the rest of Elizabeth's on-screen career, she would donate all earnings to her AIDS charities. Sometimes agreeing to do a role only if the proceeds were surrendered to her second passion in life, Richard Burton, of course, being her first.

The Poker Alice screen worn shoes

These shoes were made as part of a period gown for Elizabeth Taylor for her role in the TV movie, *Poker Alice*. The shoes are a size eight and are pink satin. Each shoe has a beautiful flower that embellishes each toe. ET is inscribed on inside of each shoe.

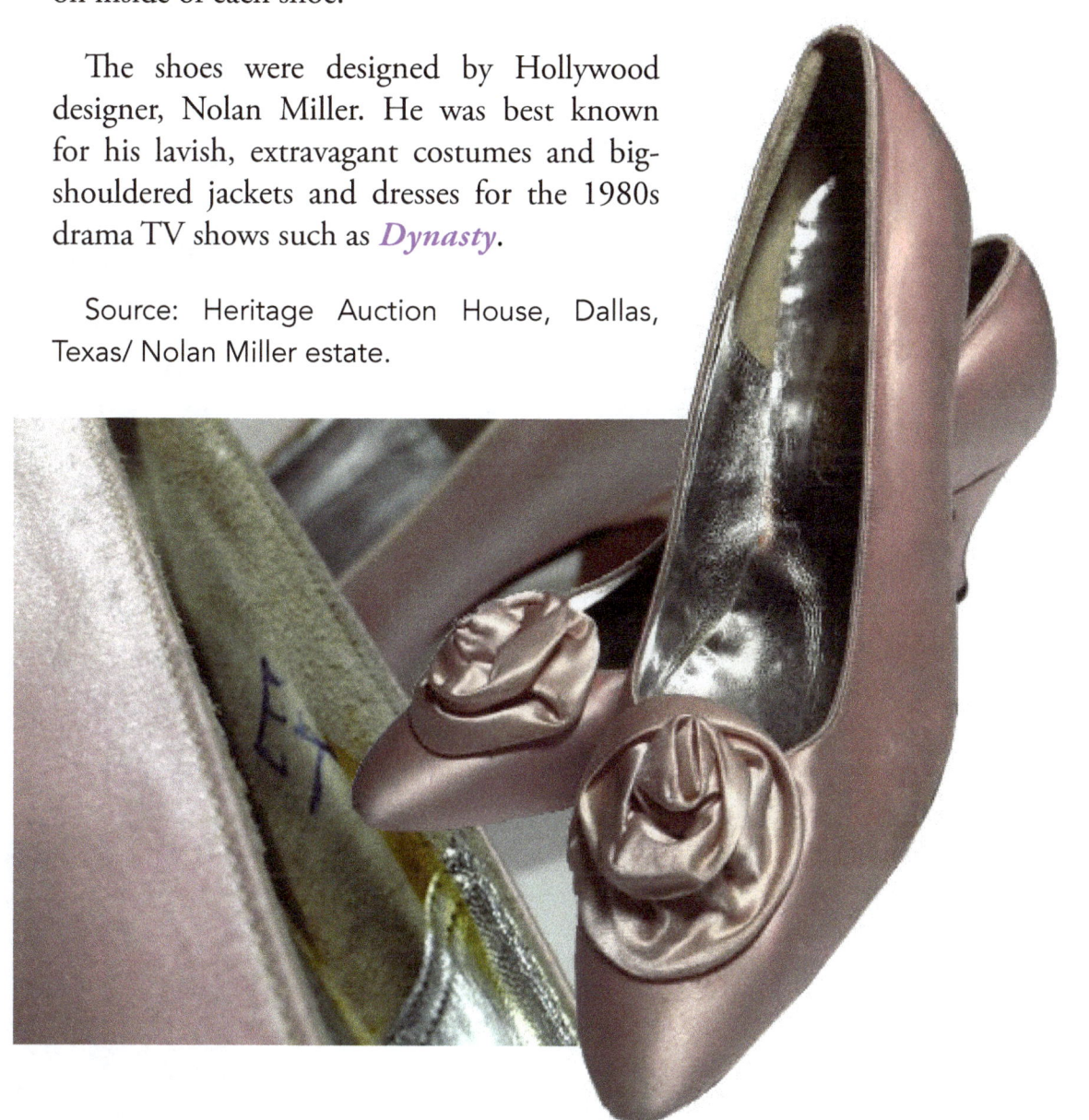

The shoes were designed by Hollywood designer, Nolan Miller. He was best known for his lavish, extravagant costumes and big-shouldered jackets and dresses for the 1980s drama TV shows such as *Dynasty*.

Source: Heritage Auction House, Dallas, Texas/ Nolan Miller estate.

The pink satin costume

This is a Nolan Miller 1870's period costume. The dress is silk satin, cotton muslin, and bobby lace. The label reads, Nolan Miller. Dress size is 4/6. This gown was worn by Dame Elizabeth Taylor in her role as Alice Moffit in the TV movie, *Poker Alice*, also starring George Hamilton.

Source: Heritage Auction House, Dallas, Texas/ Nolan Miller estate.

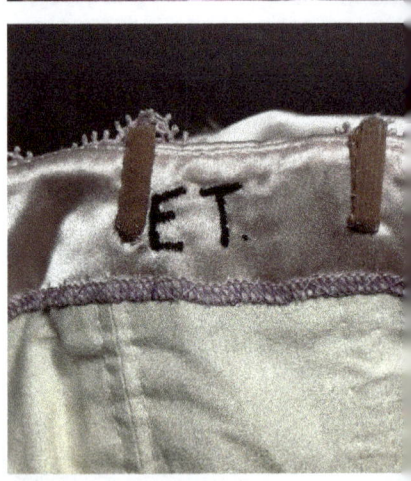

235

The deep garnet moiré taffeta costume

This gown was worn by Elizabeth Taylor in her Role as Alice Moffit in the TV movie, *"Poker Alice"*, also starring George Hamilton. The is a Nolan Miller four piece deep garnet moiré taffeta travel costume with matching hat. The jacket and skirt are taffeta moiré, satin and cotton lace. The underskirt is taffeta. The hat is velvet, taffeta moiré complimented with silk flowers, feathers, and lace. The jacket and skirt are labelled Nolan Miller. Dress size 4/6 and the hat has no size.

Source: Heritage Auction House, Dallas, Texas/ Nolan Miller estate.

237

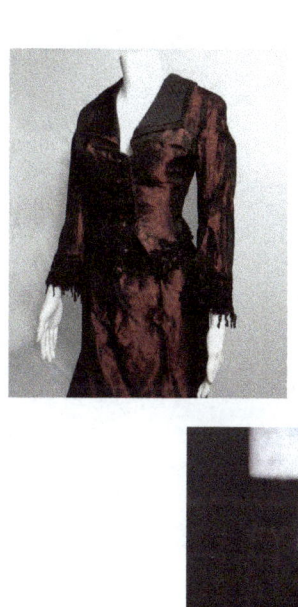

The Poker Alice faux playing cards

Robert Sheldon founder and long-time president of Old Tucson Studios first met Elizabeth in the early nineteen sixties. He shared the silver screen with Elizabeth in her role as Alice Moffat in *Poker Alice*, and after filming had ended Elizabeth gave Robert this pack of cards with one signed as a memory of their time together on the set.

Source: Robert Sheldon/Old Tuscan Studio's/Elizabeth Taylor.

Poker Alice screen worn gown

A Nolan Miller designed periwinkle blue wool and satin embroidered costume weighing 45 kilos.

Source: Antique Dress England/Nolan Miller.

The periwinkle blue wool hat

This hat was worn by Elizabeth as part of the ensemble for her role in , *Poker Alice*, 1987.

Dearest Elizabeth.....the first correspondence

After further back pain which pushed Elizabeth to excessive alcohol and drug use, she was re-admitted to the Betty Ford Centre on October 24, 1988.

Later in 1988, I sent my very first get well card to Dearest Elizabeth at the Bob Hope Drive, Rancho Mirage estate, where she had booked in under the name of 'Ruth Warner.' I called the facility to verify that Elizabeth had actually been admitted … 'We are not able to confirm or deny that Elizabeth has been admitted to this facility at this time.'

I was satisfied however that my greetings would reach my ailing starlet at this time and waited patiently for a reply. This reply would provide the essence to my thirty-year collection and the pen-friend relationship that would continue up to six months prior to Elizabeth's very sad passing in 2011.

It has been said that Elizabeth used her time in the Betty Ford facility to examine her life, her addictions, and her choices; she emerged from her rehabilitation on January 20, 1989, and had used her time to write a best seller, the dietary and self-esteem book titled, *Elizabeth Takes Off*. It provided Elizabeth with an outlet to channel her desires and also a way to tell the world that even though she was, Elizabeth Taylor, she was, in fact, human after all and had succumbed to the pressures, loneliness, and expectations of the Hollywood lifestyle.

This signed picture began my pen-friend relationship with Elizabeth, 1989.

Source: Elizabeth Taylor/Image Unknown.

Compliments of
ELIZABETH TAYLOR

Thank you for the beautiful card and gorgeous flowers!

Have a
Joyous Christmas,
and a
Wonderful New Year...
All Year!

Elizabeth Taylor

"Madonna"
Augustus John
From the Collection of
Miss Elizabeth Taylor

A Christmas card from Elizabeth to yours truly, 1988.

Source: Elizabeth Taylor.

The satin pyjamas

These beautiful orange satin pajamas were custom made for Dame Elizabeth Taylor by famed designer Andre Van Pier of Fifth Avenue. His creative influence is seen almost every day through television shows and commercials. Fashion designer Andre Van Pier died from a liver failure in the NYC hospital in August of 2008, after a long battle with Hepatitis C.

Source: Gotta Have Rock and Roll Collectibles and Andre Van Pier of Fifth Avenue.

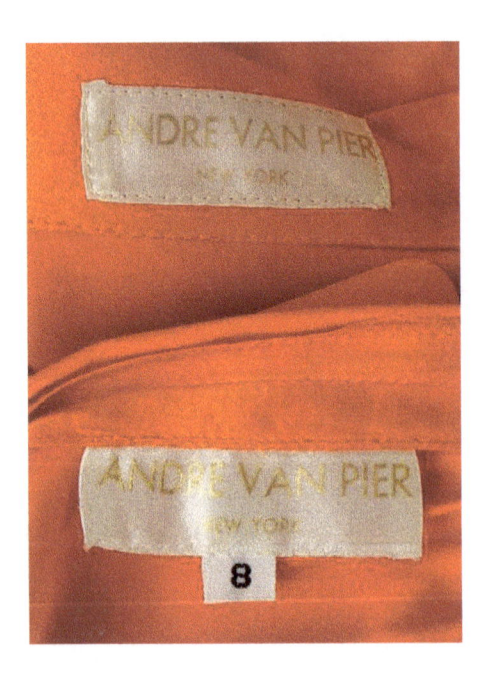

The rhinestone brooch

This is a pear-shaped brooch with teardrop inset, adorned with Austrian crystals. This brooch once belonged to Dame Elizabeth Taylor and was worn by her during a stage or movie production. After the event, Elizabeth Taylor gifted it to her longtime friend Matilda Otto.

Source: The Matilda Otto estate/ James McMahan from HeroProps4U.

Elizabeth arrives with new boyfriend, Larry Fortensky at the LA airport, 1989.

Source: Bob Scott.

'People have counted me down and out too many times. I'm a survivor and proud of it.'

- Elizabeth Taylor

Elizabeth began to regain weight and looked distracted and unhappy as she attended the American Hope Awards in March of 1989 at the Bob Hope Cultural Centre, California. The America's Hope Award was an all-star-tribute to Elizabeth's work on the big screen, but more importantly her tireless efforts in bringing awareness to AIDS.

The host of the evening was her good friend, Carol Burnett. To honour Carol Burnett in the evening, Elizabeth gave her a specially designed jacket. Carol later donated it to a charity and it became a part of this collection.

While Elizabeth may have seemed happy in the arms of her new man, she was once again facing the challenges of alcohol and drug dependency. After developing a sinus infection and fever, Elizabeth was admitted to the St Johns Hospital in Santa Monica, California on April 9, 1990. Several weeks later a lung biopsy was carried out to find the cause of what was now pneumonia.

Elizabeth was breathing with the assistance of a ventilator, her condition is serious, but stabilizing. While being reported as close to death on April 22, Elizabeth was released after her two and a half month stay at St John's Hospital.

'I am finally glad to be going home. My sole concern at this time is focused on my getting well and carrying on with my life.'

- Elizabeth Taylor

The American Hope Awards promotional jacket

This dark violet satin jacket was designed by and gifted from Elizabeth Taylor to Carol Burnett after she hosted the American Hope Awards in 1989. Elizabeth Taylor was the honored guest and recipient of the American Hope Award during the All-Star Tribute to Elizabeth Taylor. Front embroidered in gold lettering "Carol Burnett". The back embroidered: Second Annual America's Hope Awards All-Star Tribute to Elizabeth Taylor.

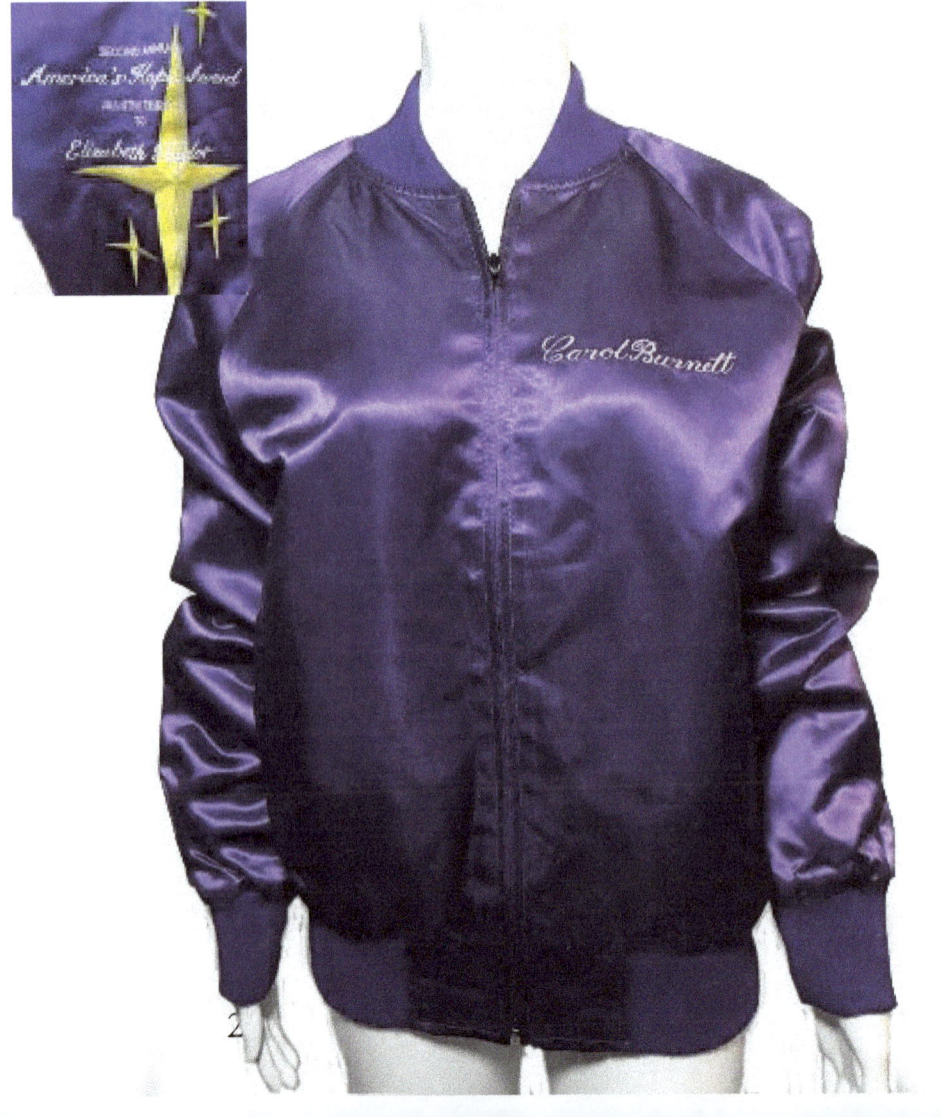

Source: Celebrity Seconds, Palm Springs, CA. USA.

Elizabeth, Larry Fortensky and Elizabeth's good friend, confidant and public relations assistant Chen Sam arrive at the Los Angeles airport, where Elizabeth appeared in court in a battle against ex-lover Henry Weinberg, who alleged that Passion, was a copy of a perfume he had developed and presented to Elizabeth, but that she had sold it as her very own, 1990. Elizabeth was awarded an undisclosed amount.

Source: Bob Scott.

In June 1991, Elizabeth was again in the courts, this time filing a claim against a US tabloid. The Tabloids published articles about Elizabeth's time spent in St John's Hospital, Santa Monica, California in April 1990. It was alleged that during her stay, Elizabeth binged on alcohol that she had smuggled into the ward. The article went on to report that Elizabeth had been placed on, 'suicide watch' and that her beautiful face was being ravaged away by Lupus. Elizabeth won yet another court battle and received the settlement she was seeking.

Quite often tabloids will often hyperbole celebrity personal life to create a scandal for their front pages. Literally: 'exaggeration' from the Greek word υπερβολή.www.wordiq. com/ definition/Hyperbola.

Elizabeth's resilience and strength to overcome this scrutiny is highly recommended and one should consider the pain to bear, a lonely one at that.

At 58, Elizabeth emerged from the Betty Ford Centre with a new lease on life, a new book and a new boyfriend, a construction worker some 20 years her junior, Larry Fortensky (Laurence Lee Fortensky) whom she met at Betty Ford while they were both on treatment Larry was good for Elizabeth, he grounded her and enabled her to be herself and do normal things like supermarket shopping.

'If all the public stopped buying the nonsense then perhaps they would all go out of business and wouldn't that just be so great.'

-Elizabeth comments on tabloid press

The relationship built between a construction worker and a Hollywood icon at the Betty Ford Centre had its ups and downs. Tabloids were reporting that it was on then it was off, Elizabeth was moving out, Elizabeth was moving in. However, nothing would prepare the world for the wedding of the year and as we have seen Elizabeth let herself go over the decades, she has always bounced back looking better than ever.

On October 6, 1991, Elizabeth married for the eight-time to Larry Fortensky some 20 years her junior. Dressed in a $30,000 Valentino designed lemon laced wedding dress and weighing only 51 kg, Elizabeth said 'I do' for the eighth time at an orchard strewn summer gazebo, built especially for the one million dollar ceremony, which was held at a good friend, Michael Jackson's Neverland estate.

'Well, I've been single for ten years.' 'I always thought - knowing my nature as a marrying kind of women - I would try, just one more time before I die.'

-Elizabeth Taylor

Elizabeth was looking fabulous at an AIDS charity, just months after her eighth marriage to Larry Fortensky.

Source: Reed Cohn.

On May 27, 1992, I actually received a reply from Chen Sam, who had been Elizabeth's public relations spokesperson for over 20 years. After years of research, years of letter writing; I was finally getting closer to the pen pal relationship that I had been longing for. In the world of celebrity, it is hard to be a fan with a difference. I knew that now that I had Elizabeth's attention I needed to maintain it. I sent a birthday card to Chen Sam to forward onto Elizabeth for her 60th birthday.

After a huge success of both men's and ladies' *Passion* fragrances in 1988-1989 Elizabeth wasted no time and released the hugely successful fragrance, *White Diamonds* in late 1992. Joining forces with Elizabeth Arden International, Elizabeth spent most of 1992 travelling and promoting her fragrances and her ongoing efforts to raise funds for her AIDS charities. She had now been away from the big screen for almost five years, making rare public appearances through her perfume advertising and the occasional AIDS charity benefit.

Her commitment to vindicating what was first known as a gay disease continued, well into the late nineties and into her final days.

The birthday napkin

This lavender coloured paper napkin was a part of the place settings for Elizabeth Taylor's 60th birthday. It is embellished in gold lettering "Elizabeth Taylor's 60th Birthday". The napkin folds up 4 inches by 4 inches. Editor Michael Arlington was a special guest at the event and was quick to retrieve Dame Elizabeth Taylor's used napkin from her place setting. Guests that attended the event were gifted with a tote bag that had a signed picture, feather mask and birthday sweater enclosed. Elizabeth Taylor sent a tote bag to the collection.

Source: Magic Kingdom, Disneyland and guest Michael Arlington.

Every guest who attended her 60th birthday bash at Disneyland received a specially designed sweater, tote bag and autographed picture of Elizabeth with her Maltese terrier 'Sugar.' Elizabeth kindly sent me the gifts to add to my collection, 1992.

Source: Disneyland/ Elizabeth Taylor.

261

Dear Wayne,

It's always a pleasure to hear from you.

Thanks a million for the wonderful T-Shirt.

Elizabeth

Elizabeth

Elizabeth and Chen Sam kept up their correspondence throughout the mid nineteen nineties.

Source: Elizabeth Taylor/Chen Sam and Associates, 1992.

The gift from Italy

These boots are knee-high black suede, adorned with five bands of rhinestone. The toes are encrusted with ten rows of rhinestones. Size 6. Boots show signs of wear. These boots were said to have been designed and gifted by Casadei of Italy for Dame Elizabeth Taylor's 60th birthday. This pair of boots were later gifted to Elliot Goodwin of Larry's Shoe Museum, Texas and then later sold to Stars Boutique. Founder of Stars Boutique Lita Sahakian is pictured with Hollywood designer, Nolan Miller.

Source: Elliot Goodwin of Larry's Shoe Museum and Stars Boutique by Lita & Co.

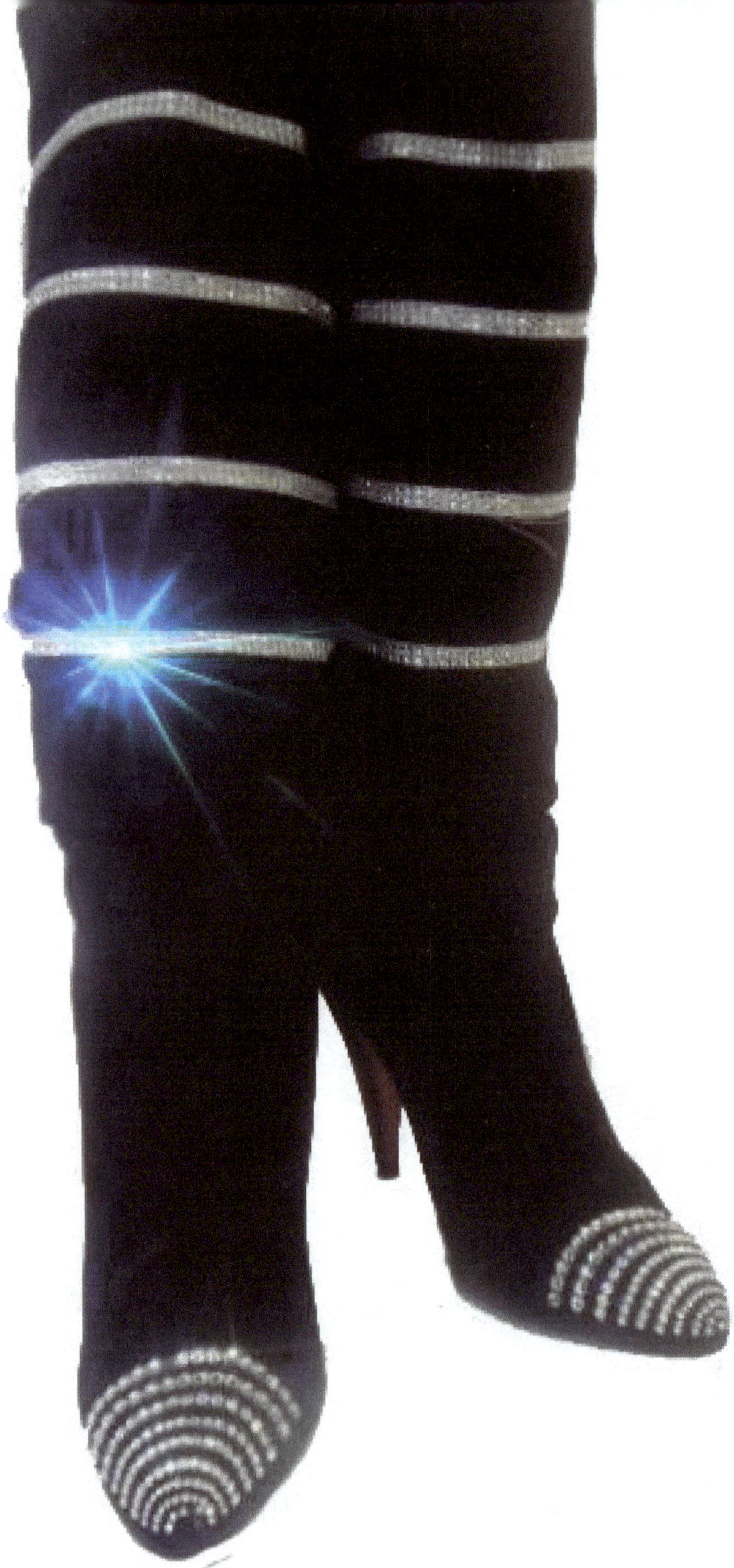

The White Diamond perfume bottle

This item was given directly to this collection by Elizabeth Taylor after I put together a portfolio of her release of *White Diamonds* in Australia 1991. After I wrote to Elizabeth Taylor and presented her with a portfolio of the marketing and presentation that accompanied the release of *White Diamonds* in Melbourne Australia, she wrote back and presented the collection with a limited edition (3000) signed perfume.

Source: Elizabeth Taylor.

Dear Wayne,

Chen Sam forwarded copies of your letters and the photographs to my home in California.

Thank you so much for being so thoughtful. I am told by my colleagues at the perfume company that the launch of White Diamonds went extremely well. I was so excited to get this news, followed by your kind letters.

I have spoken to our marketing department to see if they can assist you in obtaining a special edition bottle, and I am sure that you will be hearing from them shortly.

Hopefully one of these days I will get to Australia.

Affectionately,

Elizabeth

Elizabeth Taylor Fortensky

Confirmation from Elizabeth that I was indeed her number one fan, 1993.

Source: Elizabeth Taylor/ Herb Ritts.

On many occasions, Dame Elizabeth was unable to respond personally. Quite often I would receive autopen autographs. This is an original auto-pen that I sent back and requested a handwritten autograph.

The chiffon wrap

This is authentic glamorous, rose-pink chiffon off the shoulder evening wrap. This glamorous rose-pink chiffon wrap was used and worn by Dame Elizabeth Taylor in promotional work she did as part of her *Passion* perfume promotion. The wrap is embellished with a large rose design at the front which closes the wrap with one simple press stud. Dame Elizabeth is pictured wearing the wrap.

Source: Elizabeth Taylor estate/ Frazer's Autographs United Kingdom.

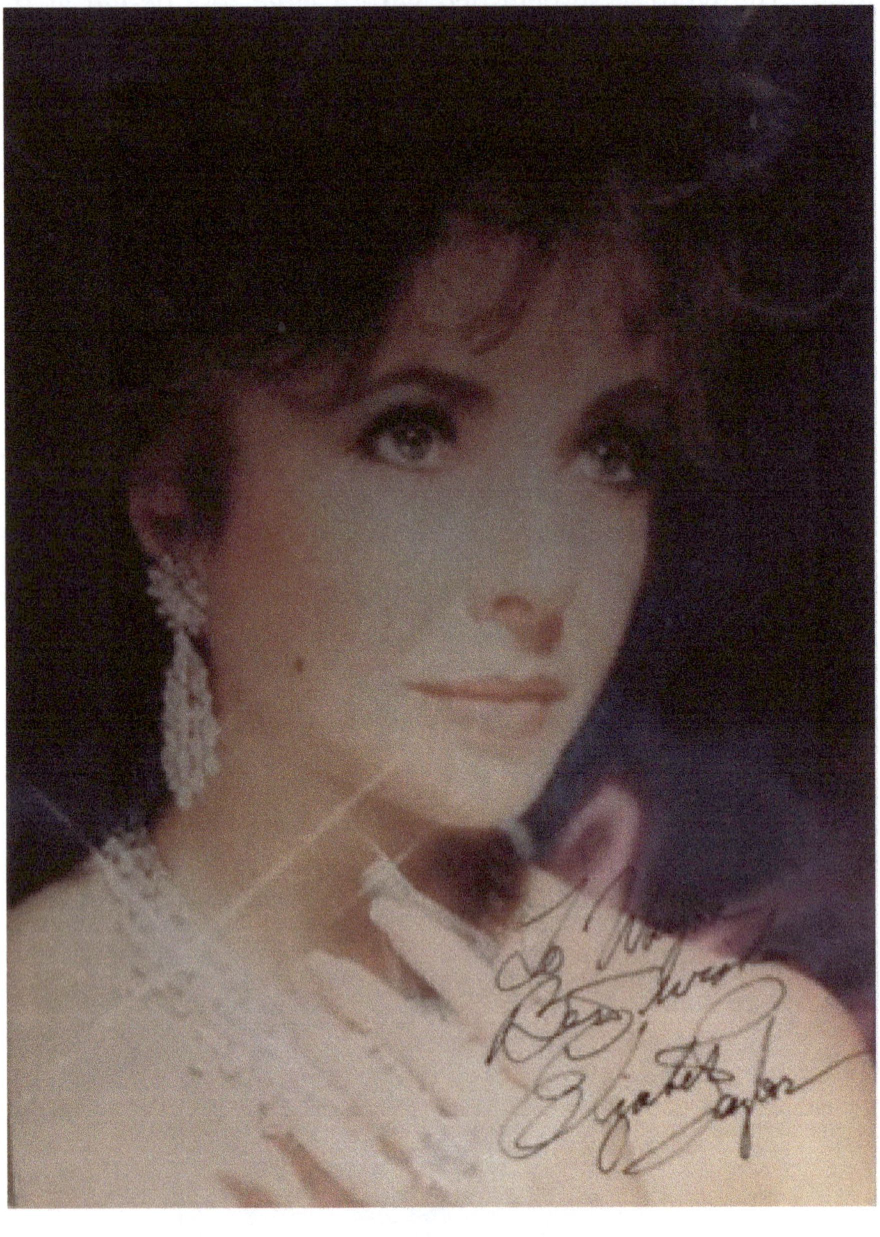

Elizabeth visits Macy's at Parma town in the US to promote her fragrances, 1993.

Elizabeth and beloved pooch Sugar on her *White Diamonds* promotional tour, 1993.

Source: Jay Nass.

> Dear Wayne,
>
> We are in receipt of your cards to Elizabeth Taylor and want you to know we are sending them directly to her.
>
> Thanks you for your thoughtfulness and good luck on your new move and future endeavors.
>
> Sincerely,
>
> *Chen Sam*
>
> Chen Sam

> Thank you for your recent letter of friendship to Miss Taylor. She is always happy to hear from her #1 fan!
>
> While we are unable to provide a personalized autograph on your photos, we are happy to send you, under separate cover, our newest publicity shot featuring Miss Taylor and Sugar, which we hope you will enjoy adding to your collection.
>
> Best wishes to you.
>
> Sincerely,
>
> Geoff Blain
> Executive Secretary to
> Elizabeth Taylor

The nineteen nineties were my most prolific corresponding years with Elizabeth, but with her work schedule sometimes quite hectic it was not always possible to correspond with her the way that a fan would perhaps like. However, Elizabeth's loyalty to her adoring public was evident on many levels and quite often there would be times that items or questions would be returned unanswered because of her unavailability to personally respond. I grew to understand celebrity protocol.

R eturning from the Cannes Film Festival Elizabeth bravely made another public appearance. While she had been bedridden since November with a severe respiratory infection, nothing was going to prevent her from being at a friend, Michael Jackson's big night at the American Music Awards.

Source: Sam Emerson.

With the sad news of her mother's passing at the age of 82 in 1994 and the recovery of her hip operation, Elizabeth was deeply depressed at the possibility that she may remain bedridden for some time. She was also faced with the task of losing 20 kilos prior to her second hip replacement later the same year.

Elizabeth and colleagues worked tirelessly in 1994 to join forces with Avon and create a line of Avon/Taylor jewelry. Elizabeth had always been a household name, now she was bringing a part of herself into the life of the average American women. Not only were her fragrances a source of inspiration, now her new line of jewelry was set to expand the Taylor Empire. Elizabeth increased the Taylor Empire and worked with Katherine Ireland to produce some amazing pieces of jewelry for her Avon collection.

After a full recovery from her hip surgery, Elizabeth made a brief cameo appearance in the June 1994 release of Steven Spielberg's film, *The Flintstones*. She agreed to do the role as long as the fee, which was 2.5 million dollars, was donated to one of her AIDS charities. After such a difficult year it was good to see Elizabeth back in all her glory on the big screen.

Elizabeth lent her voice in 1994 to *The Simpson's* character,' Maggie.' Elizabeth spoke Maggie's first words, for a donated fee of one million dollars.

'I feel my body and my spirits growing stronger; I look forward to being more active and to following my great sense of adventure and basically getting back to my world travels.'

- Elizabeth Taylor

> Dear Wayne,
>
> I am so very, very sorry to learn of the tragic loss of your partner. Please know that I will hold you close in my thoughts and in my prayers.
>
> Thank you for your kind words of condolence on the death of my mother; you are so sweet to remember me in your own time of loss.
>
> Sincerely,
>
> *Elizabeth Taylor*

Elizabeth was so very lovely to send her condolences on the death of my partner in 1994.

Source: Elizabeth Taylor.

Original promotional shoot for the newly launched Avon jewelry line, 1994.

Source: Visage Images.

From the Elizabeth Taylor jewellery collections came such pieces as the passion flower collection; the blue iridescent glass necklace; the elephant walk brooch and the amethyst encrusted ring.

Source: Visage Images.

Following the success of her previous fragrances, Elizabeth released yet another perfume in early 1996. The floral fragrance *Black Pearls*, which included spices and sandalwood, would become one of Elizabeth's most popular fragrances. Promoting her *Black Pearls* perfume range, Elizabeth made a guest appearance on four CBS sitcoms, a $250,000 deal, in a wacky story about a black pearl necklace that gets lost or stolen from show to show.

Unfortunately, her marriage to Larry Fortensky was unravelling and after a brief separation, the two divorced on 31 October 1996. It would be Elizabeth's eighth and final marriage. Setting her sights back onto her AIDS work, Elizabeth formed the *Elizabeth Taylor Aids Foundation*.

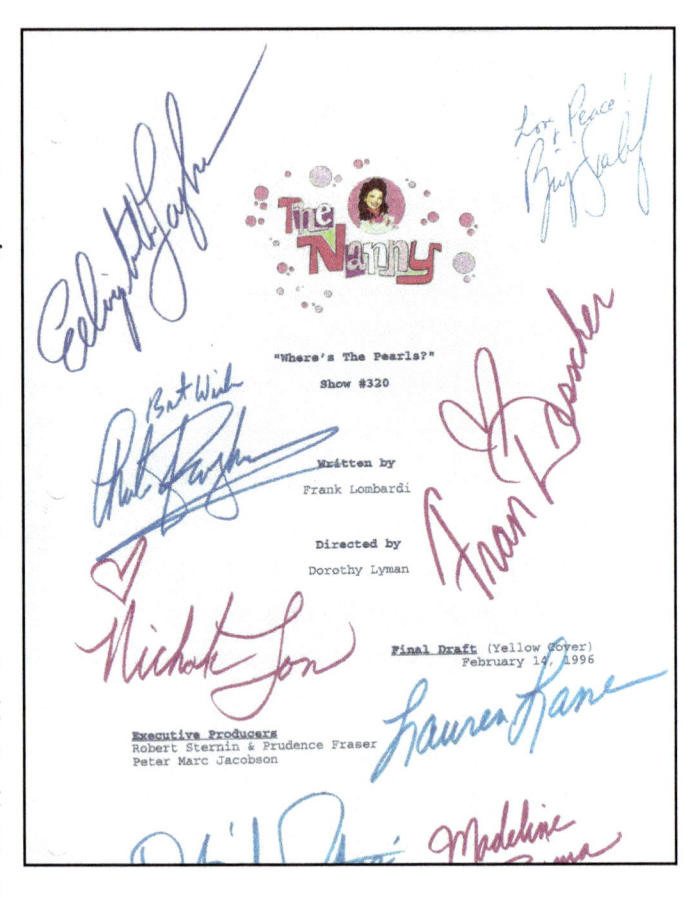

Elizabeth used her appearance on the sitcom, The Nanny, to promote her new fragrance, *Black Pearls*. Here is the script from that episode which has been signed by Elizabeth and the cast.

In the same year, Dame Elizabeth Taylor was in correspondence with Mellissa Rivers (Rosenburg) (daughter of the late Joan Rivers) co-owner of the celebrity store, "Stare Wares". Mellissa visited Nimes Road and collected 330 items Elizabeth donated t raise funds for her beloved AIDS charity.

The lavender satin and rhinestone clutch

Back in the 80s, co-founder of Star Wares, Marcia Tysseling appeared as an extra on the show "Murphy Brown". Elizabeth Taylor happens to be the guest star of the show that day and her assistant Tim, just happened to be an old friend of Melissa Rivers.

Marcia hooked up with Tim and Elizabeth Taylor invited Marcia to her home to collect several items she was willing to donate for charity. Usually, the items received from Dame Elizabeth were shoes and oddly enough vases and baskets.

When contacting Marcia, she said, "I honestly don't think she wanted her clothing sold based on insecurity of her current weight. I can totally relate and respect that. Didn't matter… I was just happy to have her as one of my consignors".

This beautiful lavender satin with a rhinestone clutch was once owned and used by Elizabeth before she donated it to raise funds for her beloved Aids charities 1996.

Source: Marcia Tysseling/ Stare Wares.

The open-toed shoes

This is a pair of open toed black and gold embossed ankle strapped Margaret J gold braided shoes from the personal wardrobe of Elizabeth Taylor. Shoes are a size 6B and formed part of the items Dame Elizabeth donated to raise funds for her beloved AIDS charity.

Source: Star Wares Collectables, California, USA.

The violet and pink belts

These two belts were part of a list of many items including hair wraps, bandanas, and scarves that were donated and the entire proceeds from the sale were to benefit *The Elizabeth Taylor AIDS Foundation*. Both belts are made by Italian designer Vaneli Vero Curio.

The first belt is leather and has been dyed pink and the second is made of leather with a lavender satin lining. The diameter of both belts is 14 inches. Dame Elizabeth Taylor is pictured here wearing a similar if not, the same pink belt.

Source: Star Wares on Main, Santa Monica, CA, USA.

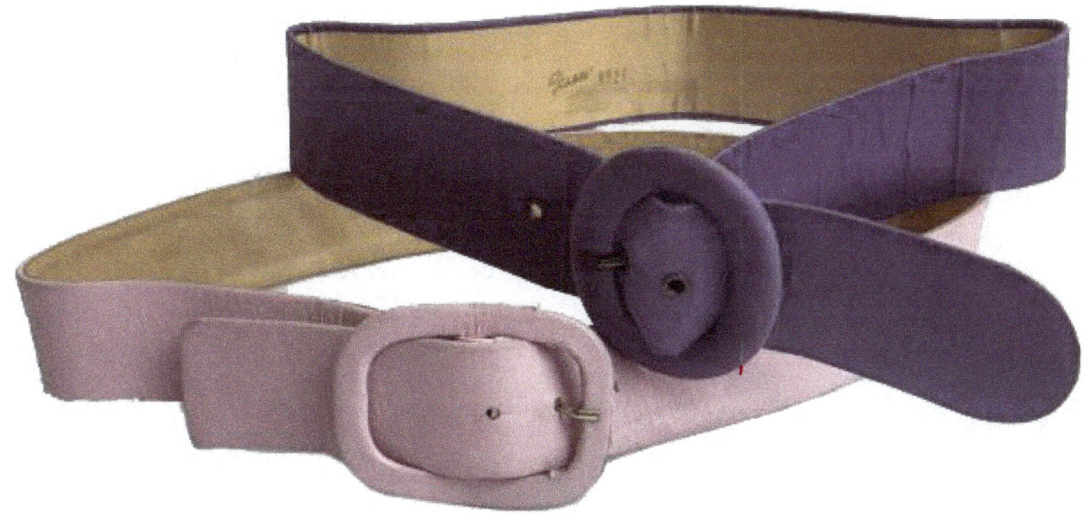

'I just don't want to do it; it would injure my sense of privacy and would hurt people who are really well known.'

- Elizabeth Taylor

Elizabeth talks about her possible autobiography.

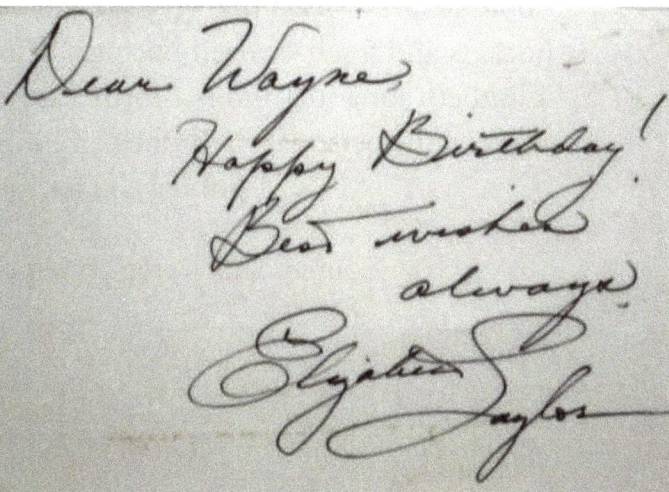

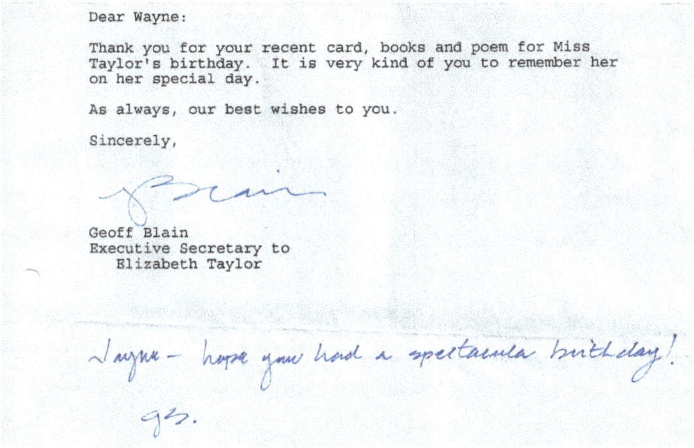

The birthday card

In 1996, I wrote to Elizabeth Taylor and informed her that whilst we had been in past correspondence, no one believed me. No one believed that I had developed a pen-friendship with the queen of Hollywood. Elizabeth took on this challenge and sent through a personal birthday greeting. One presumes she had just gone to the stationary draw, found this Vincent Van Gogh card and had her executive secretary, Geoff Blain send it.

Source: Elizabeth Taylor.

The two-piece suit

This two piece cotton cream skirt and jacket is complemented by dark blue stripes around the wrist and above the jacket hem. The jacket has welt pockets and 5 self-covered buttons. This item was created by British designers Elizabeth Emanuel and her former husband David Emanuel. It was acquired from the personal wardrobe of Elizabeth Taylor by Melissa Rivers for an animal shelter fundraising event.

Source: Star Wares on Main, Santa Monica, CA, USA.

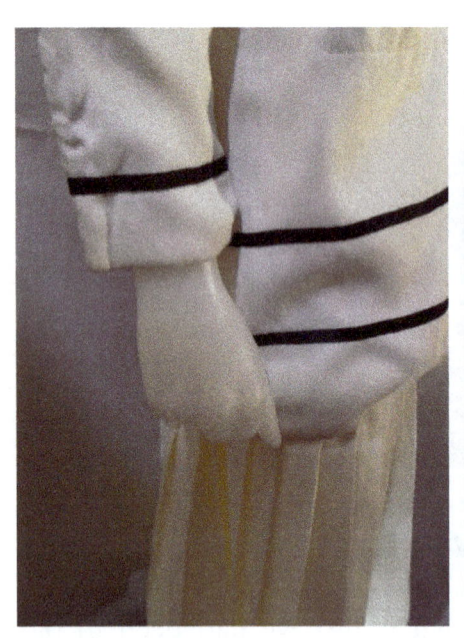

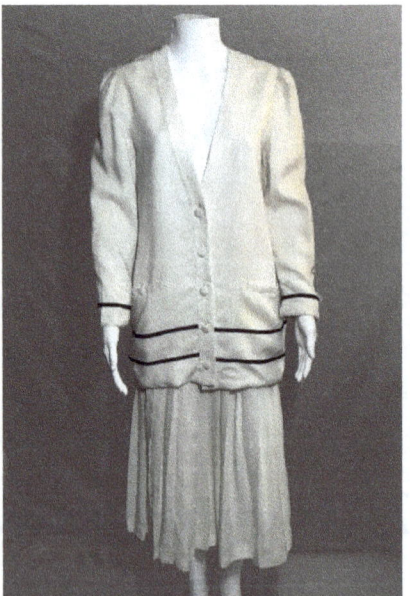

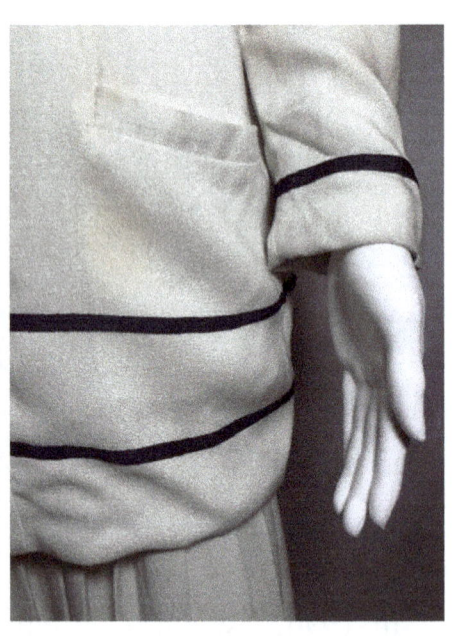

On August 26, 1996, Chen Sam, long-time companion and public relations counsel to Elizabeth passed away after a long battle with breast cancer. Chen Sam had worked closely with Elizabeth for over twenty-two years and had often dealt with yours truly on many occasions.

Grieving, Elizabeth went to Mexico.

Dame Elizabeth Taylor is pictured here with her life-long friend and confidant, Chen Sam, attending the 16th Annual Fragrance Foundation Recognition Awards at the Waldorf Hotel, New York.

Source: Bob Scott.

'Chen Sam became like a sister, the sweetest woman in the world.'

- Elizabeth Taylor

On February 15, 1997, Elizabeth was escorted on to the Pantages Theatre stage in the arms of long-time friend, Michael Jackson. The Black-tie benefit, *Happy Birthday Elizabeth, A Celebration of Life*, raised more than 1.3 million dollars for the Elizabeth AIDS Foundation.

A stretch of Hollywood Boulevard was renamed, *Elizabeth Way*, in honour of her life achievements and her 65th birthday celebration. After her birthday celebration, Elizabeth was admitted to the Cedars Sinai Medical Centre in Los Angeles where she underwent a four-hour operation to remove a five-centimetre brain tumour, which had been causing headaches and dizziness in past weeks. It was also reported that Elizabeth was also diagnosed with diabetes.

Elizabeth was surrounded by family and friends, hundreds and hundreds of bouquets and floral tributes. Elizabeth asked that instead of sending flowers or cards, donations to her AIDS foundation would be much more appreciated.

Elizabeth bears the scars from her brain tumour ordeal.

Source: Herb Ritts/Elizabeth Taylor.

Making her first public appearance since her operation, Elizabeth was looking healthy, happy and sensational with her short silver hair, as she wowed the crowds at an AIDS benefit in San Francisco. Her speech included a touching tribute to the late Princess Di and Mother Theresa.

Pictured here, Elizabeth arrived at a reception at Christie's auction house in New York, March 16, 1999.

It would not be long, however, until another mystery illness would plague Elizabeth's health, and less than a year after her brain tumour removal, Elizabeth was readmitted in January 1998 with a debilitating mystery illness, later discovered as being a nasty spinal fracture.

On my birthday, May 16, 2000, Elizabeth took centre stage at Buckingham Palace for an audience with Queen Elizabeth II, to be officially made a Dame Commander of the Order of the British Empire, the female equivalent, to a Knighthood.

Steadied on her feet, by the Queen's page and flashing the famous Taylor diamond, Elizabeth stood before the queen to receive her title for services to acting and to charity. Elizabeth's ongoing hip and back problems did not keep her from attending. Also honoured were 143 others, including Julie Andrews.

Source: Reed Cohn.

To celebrate the fact that Elizabeth was made a Dame on my birthday, Elizabeth sent me an updated autograph.

Source: Ralph Merlino.

'Me a Dame…a Dame ship, this is the most exciting … and I do not exaggerate, day of my life.'

- Elizabeth Taylor

The signed script

Whilst filming the dance number between takes, Paul Keylock got a copy of the script and asked the ladies cheekily if they could sign it undedicated. They were all darlings so Paul felt comfortable asking. The front page is signed in a variety of colours by the four leading ladies. Paul Keylock was the personal assistant to Joan Collins on the set of *These Old Broads*.

The script was written by the late Carrie Fisher.

Source: Paul Keylock.

Elizabeth appeared as a special guest at her friend Michael Jackson's family honour celebrations at Madison Square Garden, New York, September 10, 2001.

Source: Reed Cohn.

In 2001 Elizabeth was still on the celebrity perfume trail and released her floral mix of carnation, Bulgarian rose and mandarin orange in true Taylor style. *Sparkling Diamonds* became another huge hit for the legendary actress.

A musical celebration in her honour was held at the Royal Albert Hall in England May 26, 2001.

In October of 2001, Elizabeth teamed up with Hollywood sirens of the silver screen, Joan Collins, Debbie Reynolds, and Shirley McLain in a TV film comedy, due for release in early 2002. *These old Broads* was written by Debbie Reynolds daughter Carrie Fisher, is a story of three aging divas that, reluctantly reunite to make a TV series.

Over 40 years ago, Elizabeth married Debbie Reynolds's husband in a bid to keep the ghost of her third husband, Mike Todd alive, after his sudden death in a plane crash in 1958. The get together of *These Old Broads* was a real-life testament that the two had perhaps finally put the scars from the past behind them. Elizabeth played the role of a burnt out agent, a part that required very little of Elizabeth, the role was specially written to accommodate Elizabeth's frail back.

By the end of 2001, Elizabeth had raised more than 600 million dollars for AIDS research.

Elizabeth still maintained her relationship with her number one fan, 2001.

Source: Reed Cohn.

Beautiful image of Elizabeth signed in silver pen.

Source: Elizabeth Taylor/ Bruce Weber.

> Charla Lawhon
> Managing Editor, *In Style*
>
> Invites you to celebrate
>
> ELIZABETH TAYLOR
> MY LOVE AFFAIR WITH JEWELRY
> published by Simon & Schuster
>
> Join Dame Elizabeth Taylor and view an exclusive exhibition of selected jewels from her legendary private collection.
>
> Cocktail Party
> Thursday, September 26th, 2002
> 6:30 pm to 9:30 pm
> Festive cocktail attire
>
> Christie's
> 20 Rockefeller Plaza
> (49th Street between Fifth and Sixth Avenues)
> New York City
>
> R.S.V.P. by September 16th
> 212.522.8349
>
> THIS INVITATION IS NON-TRANSFERABLE
> PHOTO IDENTIFICATION REQUIRED

Ailing Elizabeth had now become a Hollywood recluse and was confined to a wheelchair. She did, however, compile a beautiful book on the collection of her jewelry titled, *Elizabeth My love affair with jewelry*. Elizabeth sent me an invitation to attend an exclusive exhibition of jewelry from her private collection.

On the evening of Thursday, September 26, 2002, Elizabeth held a private launch of her new book at her Belair mansion and this was the only time she signed copies of her new book. A very good friend of hers, who was a close friend to her executive secretary Mr. Geoff Blain, obtained this signed copy from Elizabeth on the night. Elizabeth did not make public appearances or book signings due to her ill health at the time.

Elizabeth inscribes a message to her doctor on the inside of another copy her new book 'my beloved Arnie I love you more than I could tell- I feel you have saved my fading life, I love and thank you forever, yours Elizabeth T.'

At the age of 71, Elizabeth finally bid farewell to show business after 60 years and was to join a line-up of past Oscar winners as part of celebrations to mark the Academy's 75th anniversary, Elizabeth declined the invitation. Media reports suggested that Elizabeth was now settling into semi-retirement and would often remind herself of her heyday by playing some of her old favourite movies at home with friends and family. *Who's Afraid of Virginia Woolf?* and *A Place in the Sun* were said to be among her favourites.

On the odd occasion, she would venture out, with the help of her personal assistants, to attend fundraisers and collect accolades for past and present works, including her Presidential Citizens Medal presented to her at the White House, one of the final honour ceremonies of the Bill Clinton presidency.

The success of Elizabeth's fragrances has inspired and motivated not only thousands of women worldwide but has also encouraged other celebrities to launch fragrances of their own.

In 2003, Elizabeth released two fragrances *Gardenia* and *Forever Elizabeth*. The name of which I believe came from the signing off of my correspondence, *Forever Elizabeth*, your number one fan.

Elizabeth signs off on what has been reported as the largest collection of its kind in the world, 2003.

Source: Albany Advertiser, Western Australia.

Pure intensity and brilliance

In 2003, Dame Elizabeth Taylor shades of violet- a story told in memorabilia was recognised by the Australian Collector's Association as being the 'Best Displayed' collection on show and was also awarded the 'People's Choice Award' for its pure intensity and brilliance.

At 74, Elizabeth to some had appeared to age very quickly over the past few years. Her image had disappeared from magazines and papers that had haunted her every move. Plagued with health problems all her life, along with her on and off drug and alcohol dependency, it would appear that it was all catching up to her.

Continued reports of her being on her death bed were flashed around the world, it's hard to imagine ready your own obituary, but this was something Elizabeth had done many times before. Taking up the challenge, Elizabeth appeared on the Larry King show, which would be her first television interview in over four years. Being pronounced death four times in the past, Elizabeth wanted everyone to know that in fact, she was very much alive.

In 2006, Elizabeth signed a deal with Christie's Auction House, giving them exclusive rights to handle future sales of her jewelry, artworks, memorabilia, clothing, and other personal possessions. The auction house had previously sold gowns and jewelry, including the 1986 Academy Award dress which was part of this collection. The proceeds were to benefit the *Elizabeth AIDS foundation* and the *American Foundation for AIDS research* (Am FAR).

My correspondence with Elizabeth had wavered off to perhaps one or two letters or autographs a year. I was getting the stage where I thought I would honour Elizabeth in her twilight years and let her enjoy the reclusiveness that sometimes I think she longed for.

Reports in July of 2008 suggested that Elizabeth was admitted to hospital and placed on life support after she had been diagnosed with heart failure and a severe bout of pneumonia. Once again reports of Elizabeth being on her death bed were denied by her publicist, who implied that her health problems were exaggerated and that Elizabeth's visit to the hospital was a mere precaution. Of late she had become a regular at Abbeys gay bar and restaurant, California. Quite often she was seen sitting with friends enjoying a lime Daiquiri or two.

'Elizabeth is the best old school dame I've ever met.' 'A regular, wonderful person, boy did I take to her, she's an astonishing great broad.'

- Johnny Depp

The white silk handkerchief

This silk handkerchief was owned and used by Dame Elizabeth Taylor. The handkerchief is appliqued "Elizabeth" in green.

Source: Elizabeth Taylor estate by R&R Enterprises, Bedford, NH, USA.

The denim hat

Collector Barry Weiss was invited to Elizabeth Taylor's estate after her passing in 2011 and procured this denim hat that remained in the bottom of Elizabeth Taylor's wardrobe. He informed me that Elizabeth's people were most kind during the transaction. Unfortunately, he was required to sign a confidentiality contract and was unable to share any other information. Elizabeth is seen here wearing similar if not the same hat in 2009.

Barry Weiss first came to the public attention as the eccentric collector in the reality television series "Storage Wars"

Source: Barry Weiss/ Elizabeth Taylor estate/ Barcroft Media.

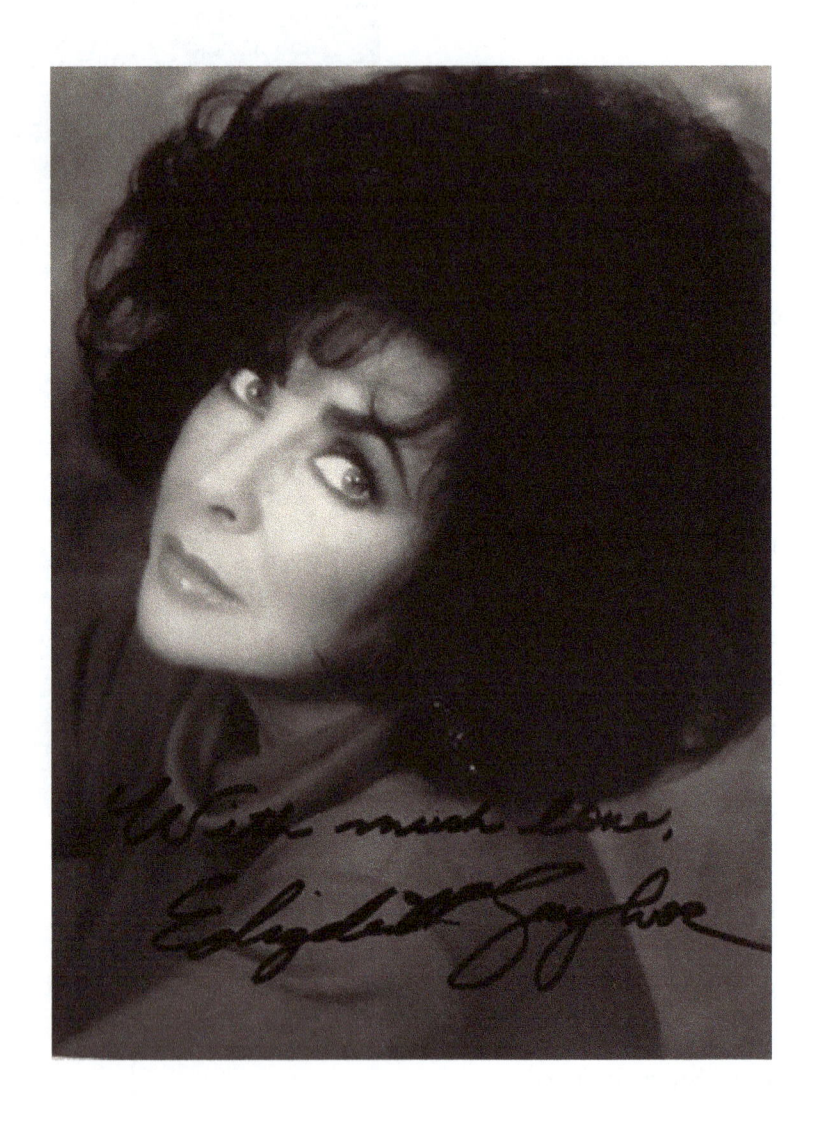

T his was the last signed photograph I received from Elizabeth, and I was shocked to see her beautiful signature resemble the scribble of an elderly lady, but unlike her written hand. Elizabeth had aged so very gracefully, this was no act; this was Elizabeth in her truest essence.

Source: Harry Benson/Elizabeth Taylor.

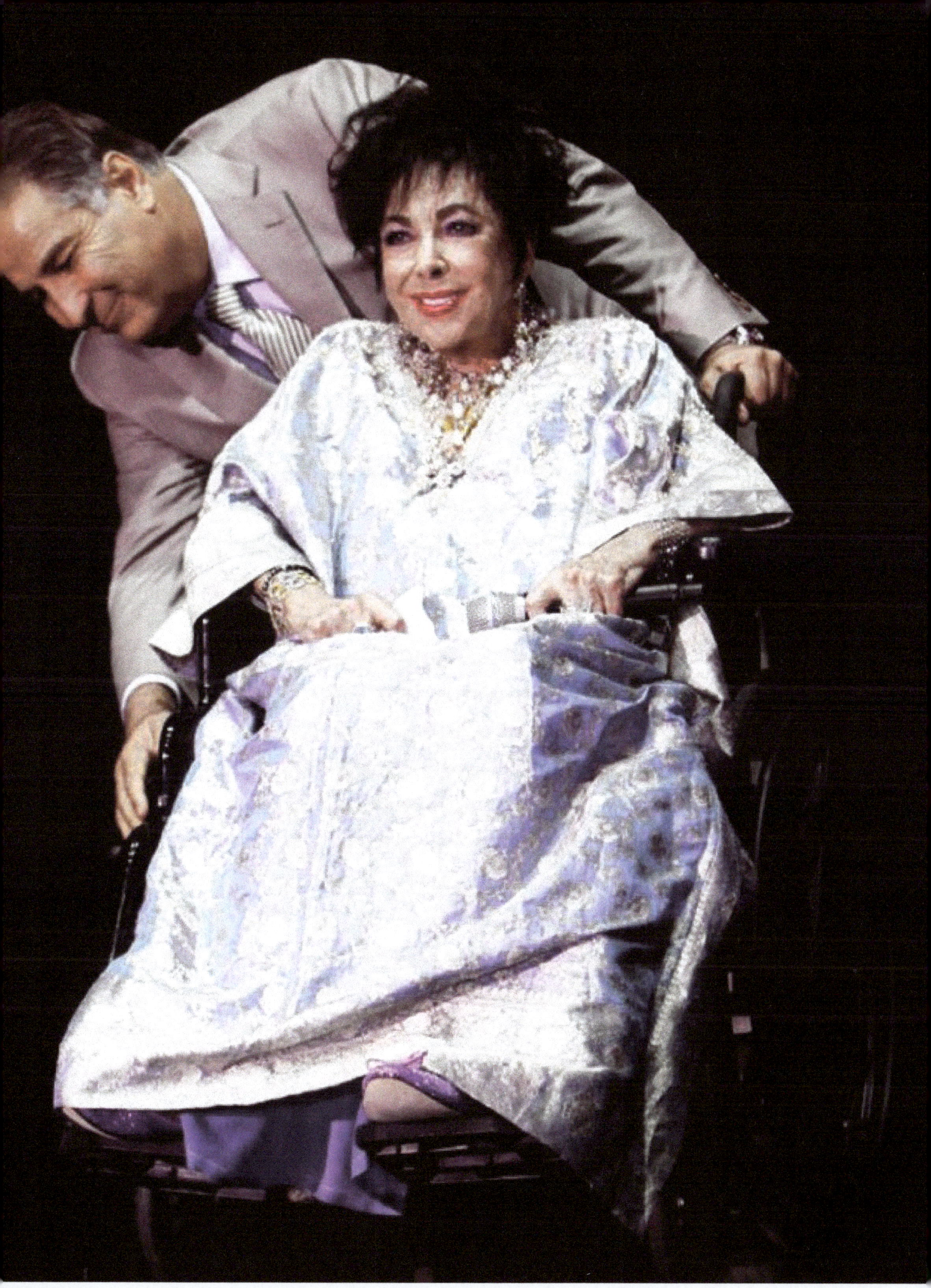

The lavender manuscript

In February 2010, I decided that it was time for Elizabeth to receive the very first manuscript of this collection. It was also a way of closing the book on what some have described as a lifelong obsession, but I like to refer to it as a lifetime friendship. I sent the original five hundred and ninety-one page manuscript which was bound in lavender satin. It left Australia for America on February 15, 2010. An email from House of Taylor informed me of its arrival on 25 February, just two days before Elizabeth's 78th birthday.

In the meantime, on September 22, 2010, Eddie Fisher aged 82 died from complications during hip surgery. He was Elizabeth's 4th husband.

In November 2010, I received Elizabeth's response to this book and was overwhelmed that in the entire world she still managed to find me, she still managed to surprise me and we still had our pen-friend relationship. I now lived from day to day with tabloid press feeding me images and headlines that would tell me that Elizabeth was at her end. Just like all the other times, these scavengers had prayed on the misfortunes of others by printing scandalous headlines. I prayed that again they would be wrong.

'I have lived with people speculating about my health all my life and I don't say this with sarcasm but sadly, I have outlived so many who have prematurely buried me. There are so many other things in this world to worry about and that are much more important than my health.'

- Elizabeth Taylor

> Dear Wayne,
>
> Thank you for thinking of me on my birthday and sending along the lovely lavender tribute book, which brought back so many memories. You are so thoughtful to take the time to compile such an extensive volume.
>
> You made my day very special with this lovely gift. Best wishes to you.
>
> Sincerely,
>
> *Elizabeth Taylor*

The final letter

After viewing the original manuscript of this book, Elizabeth would write to me for the very last time, November 20, 2010.

'If I wasn't dead every two weeks the tabloids wouldn't make any money.'

- Elizabeth Taylor

The final shade of violet

In 2011, I followed the internet every day after I heard that Elizabeth had been admitted to the Cedars-Sinai Medical Centre (Hospital to the stars) on Friday, February 11, 2011, for treatment of congestive heart failure. Elizabeth was reported as doing well and her publicist and close family appreciated the ongoing support of fans but had asked they provide privacy at this time to allow the medical team space to do their work.

It was unknown how long Elizabeth now 78 and very frail would be admitted. Elizabeth had been using a wheelchair for the past five years to cope with chronic back ailments after breaking her back four times, of course, the first time was when she was 12 in the movie that would change her life forever, National Velvet, 1945. Elizabeth had had three hip replacements, a benign tumour removed, skin cancer and pneumonia four times plus the countless times she had been admitted to hospital for other ailments.

Elizabeth was reported as still being in the hospital for two weeks and spent her 79th birthday bedridden. This would be my last bouquet of flowers I would send to her bedside.

On March 15 2011, Elizabeth was entering her second month at Cedars-Sinai Medical Centre. I was putting the final touches to this book, which was to be a celebration of a memorabilia collection that was to honour Elizabeth, when at 1:20 am on March 23 I received a text message which read, 'Wayne so sorry to hear about your Dearest Elizabeth.'

I had had these messages before because of people's response to tabloid lies. I immediately got out of bed and jumped online. Only to read that yes, Elizabeth Taylor had passed away in her sleep at 1:28 am USA time 23 March 2011. I could not go back to bed, I could not sleep so I put on, *Who's Afraid of Virginia Woolf?* If Elizabeth had passed away I was certain that she and Richard Burton would have been making the sequel, Who's Afraid of Virginia Woolf? I received numerous texts all day and phone calls. I guess people that knew me would know how devastated I was. Elizabeth has been a big part of my life.

Showing a sense of humour to the end, Elizabeth made her final grand entrance in true movie star style when she arrived 15 minutes late to her own funeral. Elizabeth was buried at Forest Lawns cemetery in Glendale, California in a quiet service. Her swift burial was due to Jewish Tradition, if you remember she was converted to Judaism when she married husband Eddie Fisher. Her grandson played Amazing Grace on his trumpet and the world mourned the loss of the last Hollywood legend.

There was no public memorial but instead, a worldwide exhibition of Elizabeth's famous costumes and jewels, which were later, auctioned to raise funds for her beloved Aids charities at Christies in New York. The Christies auction raised more than 680 million dollars for *The Elizabeth Taylor Aids Foundation*.

'We have just lost a Hollywood giant. More importantly, we have lost an incredible human being'

- Sir Elton John

Dame Elizabeth's star on the Hollywood Walk of Fame is adorned with floral tributes after the world received the news of her sad passing. The Hollywood Walk of Fame comprises more than 2,500 five-pointed terrazzo and brass stars embedded in the sidewalks along 15 blocks of Hollywood Boulevard and three blocks of Vine Street in Hollywood, California.

Credit: RoidRanger / Shutterstock.com

Every World Aids Day not only will the world remember those that are suffering a life-threatening illness, but they will forever remember Dearest Elizabeth, the pioneering activist whose face can be seen behind every red ribbon.

World Aids Day, Melbourne, Australia, 2013.

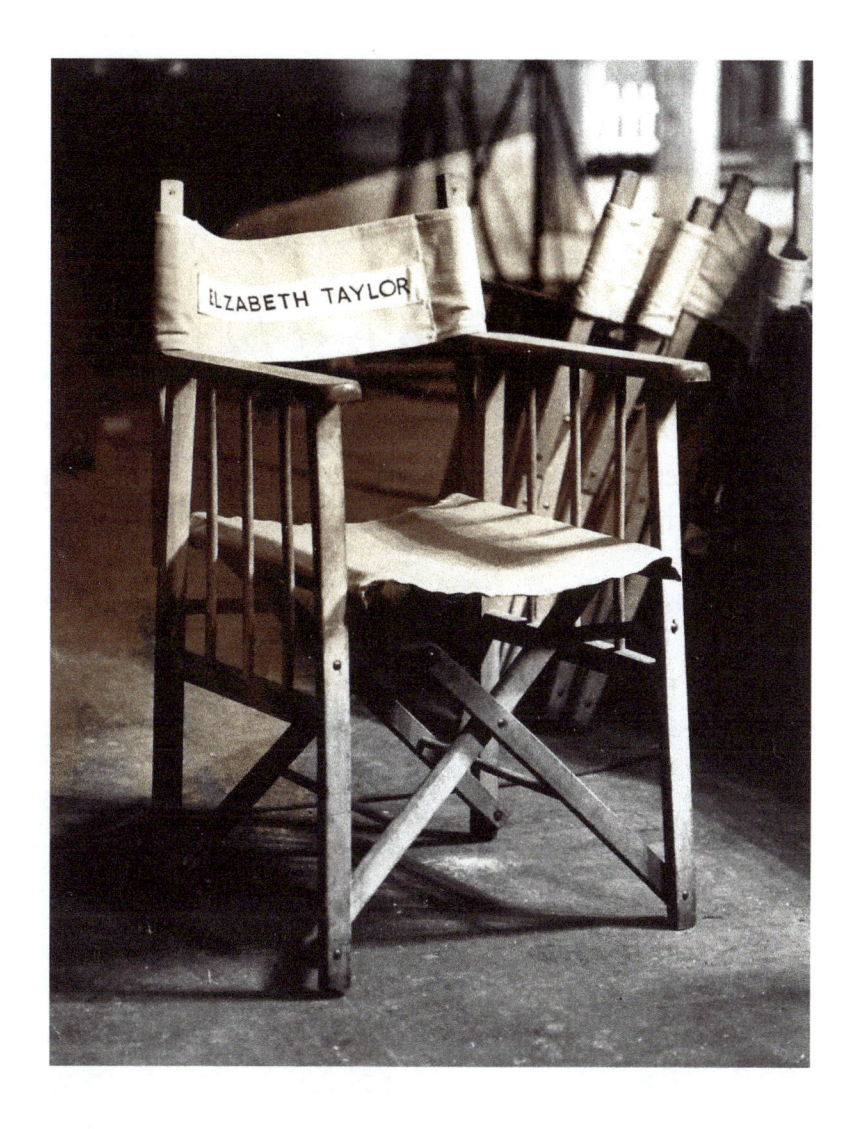

A half-hearted attempt to bring both Elizabeth and Richard back to the big screen ended as quickly as it began. The telemovie titled 'Liz and Dick' co-stared the troubled actress, Lindsay Lohan and only re-enforced the fact that there could only ever be one Elizabeth. There will never be another star so bright; there will never be another woman with so much strength and dignity, there will never be a super star so real. This book, this collection is the truest testament of the admiration the world did and will always have for Hollywood's Dame Elizabeth Taylor.

Once Elizabeth and Richard would sit together on the set of one of their movies, now these seats would only be a reminder of what used to be.

Source: International magazine service 1963.

Dame Elizabeth rest in peace

At Glendale Elizabeth and Michael Jackson share this arch where they both now rest in peace. Elizabeth rests peacefully with a love letter from the love of her life, Richard Burton.

Source: Forest Lawn, Glendale, California/ Deidre and Gael.

The largest memorabilia auction in history

Several months after her passing Elizabeth Taylor would have Christies Auctions of New York host the largest memorabilia auction in history. Funds raised from auctioning off memorable and personable Elizabeth Taylor items, from her wardrobe, her estate, and her famous jewelry collection would be donated to her lifelong charity, *The Elizabeth Taylor Aids Foundation*.

The Elizabeth Taylor auction shattered all previous auction records. The first night of the spectacular auction saw the sale of some of Elizabeth's prized jewelry pieces, which fetched over $116 million dollars. This set a world record for a private collection of jewels.

A definite highlight of the auction was the sale of Mike Todd's diamond tiara which sold for a staggering 4.2 million dollars, smashing its expected estimate of $80,000.

However, the winner of the night was the most famous pearl in history "La Peregrina," the 16th Century pearl on a necklace designed by Cartier for Elizabeth sold for $11.8 million, setting the world record for a pearl jewel.

In a separate auction of items from the legends personal wardrobe, a total of 67 lots were sold, reaching another record, this time in fashion auctions. The fashion auction raised an incredible 2.6 million dollars. The item that raised the most interest and was the most expensive was the silver encrusted brocade Christian Dior and matching purse. It sold for $362,500.

The Collection of ELIZABETH TAYLOR

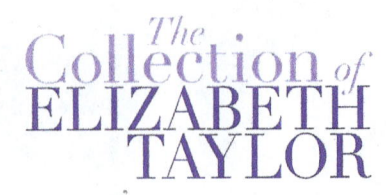

Thank you
*for your recent purchase from
The Collection of Elizabeth Taylor.*

For more information on Christie's auctions please visit us at
www.christies.com.

For any questions regarding your purchase please contact us at
212 468 7199 or elizabethtaylorcollection@christies.com.

CHRISTIE'S

ET

CHRISTIE'S

Source: Christies Auctions/Elizabeth Taylor.

My homage to Dame Elizabeth Taylor

During my pen-friendship with Elizabeth, I was provided with several opportunities to meet with the Queen of Hollywood but was unable to attend due to a variety of reasons. In 2015 I decided that I would pay homage to Elizabeth Taylor and I made a special trip to Los Angeles. I visited her gravesite at the Glendale Forest Lawn Memorial Park, took a stroll down the Hollywood walk of fame and another stroll through the faux gates of Belair. Going to visit the house Elizabeth purchased in the early 1980's and lived in until her passing was a huge sensory experience. When the gates of her former home opened my senses were overwhelmed by the exotic equatorial and sweet smells of jasmine and gardenia. It was like Elizabeth Taylor had herself, just sashayed through the gates.

I left a copy of this book with the new property owners thinking that a part of me had finally somehow been allowed to embrace the corridors of Elizabeth's Belair estate.

> Picture: The corridor at the Forest Lawn Mausoleum where both Elizabeth Taylor and Michael Jackson have been put to rest. Elizabeth under the 20 foot angel and Michael at the end of the corridor, under the circular glass stained window.

ACS security services officer, Walter, permits access to the Belair compound. I got talking to him and he informed me that he has been a security officer at the Bel air compound for over 25 years. He went on to tell me that Elizabeth Taylor was always so pleasant and would often wave if she saw him at the faux gates.

The entrance to Belair.

Dame Elizabeth's former entrance to her last place of residence, 700 Nimes Rd Belair LA, California.

Dame Elizabeth's favourite cocktail

I knew then I had achieved what I had set out to achieve, so I made my way to Elizabeth's favourite bar. I sat in the same seat Elizabeth would sit during her visits to the Abbey Bar and Grill. As I ordered a cocktail made especially for Elizabeth's visit a large ray of sunlight beamed through the coloured leadlight glass. It was like she had come to join with me in finally celebrating our connection. I was lucky enough also to acquire the recipe to a drink designed for Elizabeth and drank by her on her last visit.

Dame Elizabeth Taylor- shades of violet

- Premium Vodka 20 oz

- Kurant/ Berry Schnapps 50 oz.

- Fresh lemon juice 10 oz.

- Sugar syrup Float Blue curacao

- Serve in large martini glass.

- Garnish with fresh blueberries and raspberries.

A visit to Dame Elizabeth's star on the Hollywood Walk of Fame.

A visit to the Friars Club New York

The Queen of Celebrity Activism

In 2017, parts of this private collection which have been gathered over a 30-year friendship with Elizabeth was exhibited. Once upon a time the word 'Star' applied to someone fabulous who worked in the entertainment industry. It was an accolade given to someone with magnetism, glamour and a quality that set them apart from mere mortals. Elizabeth Taylor was in every sense of the word a Super Star.

Elizabeth Taylor also had a passionate commitment to fighting HIV/AIDS and, in 1985, began donating her personal income as well as raising funds to discover a cure. Today her efforts continue posthumously and contribute significantly to the cause. The legacy of her unwavering and tireless work will surpass the likes of any Kardashian or any other wannabe celebrity heads. Elizabeth Taylor's passion in her later years was her involvement with both the American Foundation for AIDS Research and her own foundation, The Elizabeth Taylor Aids Foundation.

"It's the most important work of my life," she once said, and Elizabeth's unwavering energy proves this is no idle boast.

The exhibition showcased some of Elizabeth's prized personal effects, collectable items and pieces that will give an insight into the entertainer and the activist.

326

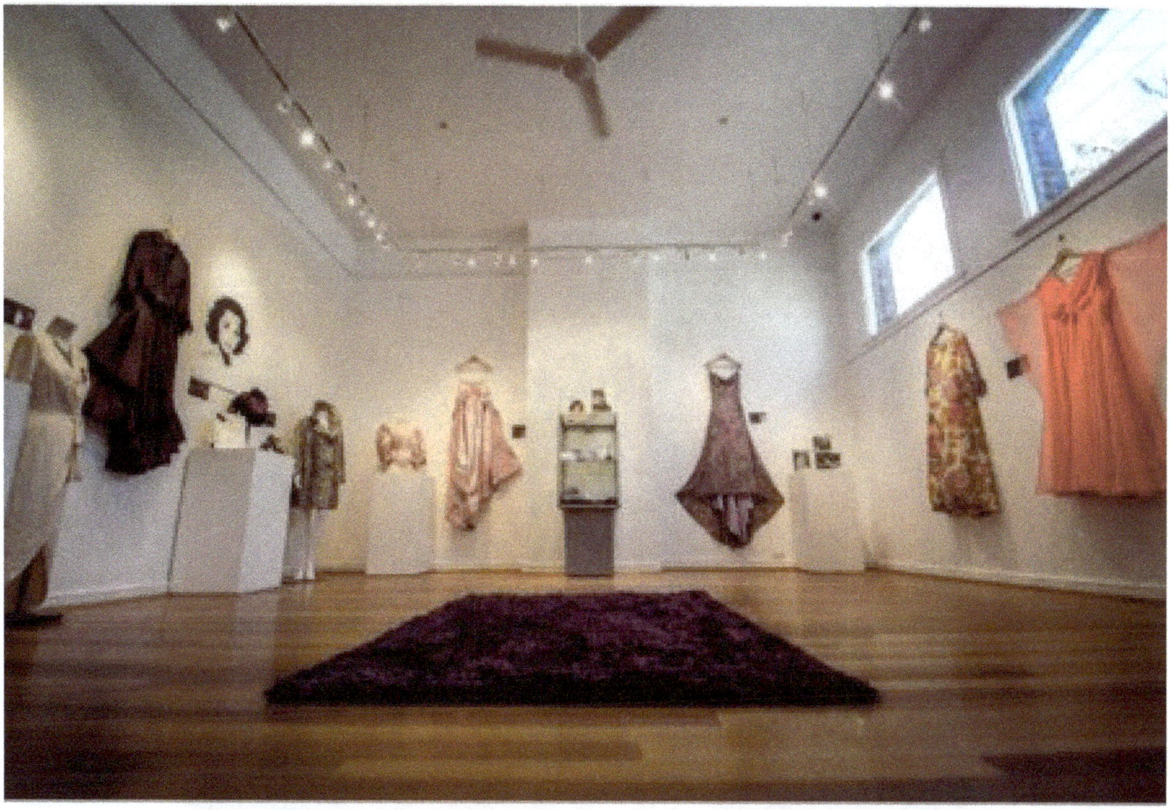

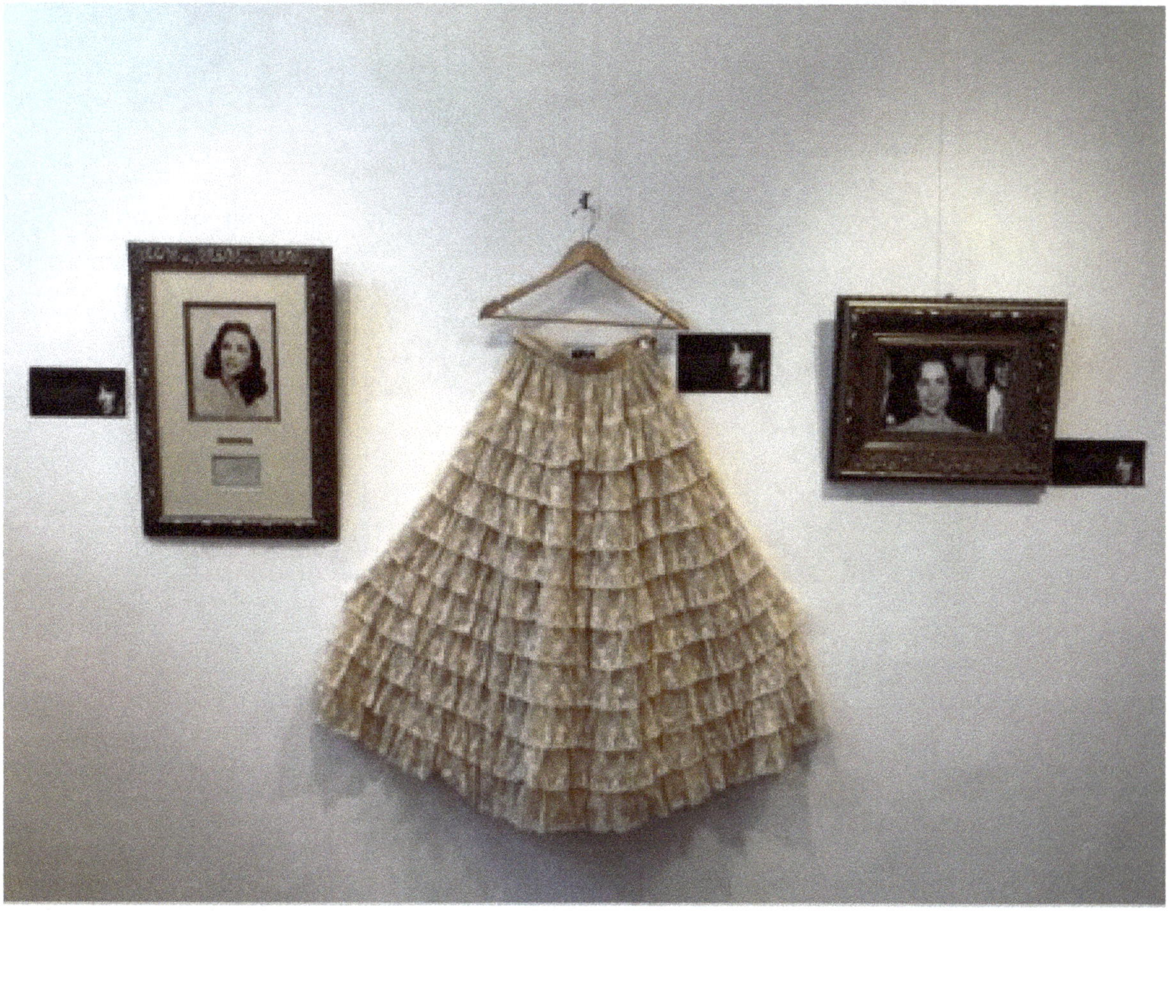

#midsumma at gasworks arts park
Elizabeth Taylor
FREE ENTRY
OPEN LATE ON MIDSUMMA SHOW NIGHTS
THE QUEEN OF CELEBRITY ACTIVISM
17 JANUARY TO 5 FEBRUARY 2017 • 9.30AM TO 5PM
VISUAL ART EXHIBITION • ANGELA ROBARTS BIRD GALLERY
CELEBRATING HER PASSIONATE COMMITMENT TO FIGHTING HIV / AIDS
TOLD THROUGH A PRIVATE COLLECTION OF HER PERSONAL EFFECTS
JOY
MIDSUMMA FESTIVAL

'Isn't this what being a celebrity is all about, helping people?'

– Elizabeth Taylor

Dame Elizabeth Taylor is immortalised in shades of violet at the Madame Tussaud's Wax Museum Las Vegas, Nevada, USA.

'Give, remember always give. That is the thing that will make you grow.'

– Elizabeth Taylor

Since her passing in 2011, Ms. Taylor's friends and family continue to work tirelessly together as ETAF ambassadors to support HIV/AIDS issues and maintain worldwide awareness. Dame Elizabeth Taylor's legacy of work continues through the unwavering efforts of The Elizabeth Taylor AIDS Foundation.

Keep Elizabeth's legacy alive and donate at:
www.elizabethtayloraidsfoundation.org/

"I hope with all my heart that in some way I have made a difference in the lives of people with AIDS. I want that to be my legacy"

Photographic credits

Tom Wargacki - Nancy Barr - Seuss Filtio - Ralph Merlino - Charles Moniz - Brad Darrach - Robert Cohen - Lou Valentino - Erika Davidson - Joe Decker – Neal Peters- Nat Gallinger - Yani Begakis - Elis McCarthy - Reed Cohen - Frank Teti - Kevin Winter - Chris Hunter - Herb Ritts -Bob Scott - James Smeal - Peter Brandt - Alex Berliner - Cal Gleason -Gene Daniels - Henry Pessar - Marcus Adams - Beverly Carr - Nancy Barr -Sam Emerson -Bruce Weber- Harry Winston - Floyd McCarty - Felice Quinto - Clarence S Bull - Danny Eccleston - Raimondo Borea - Jack Buxbaun - Michael Tullberg - Ethan Miller- Vincent Yu Slug- Fred Guiol.

Special resources

Star Wares, Celebrity Seconds, Heritage Auction House, Julien's Auction House, and Fraser's Autographs, George Houlle Books and autographs, Video Connection, Wholesale video supplies, Warner Home Video. Communication and Entertainment limited, Hoyts Polygram Video, Road show home video library, Columbia Pictures, Twentieth Century Fox, Stars, rock and Movie Posters.

Museum of moving images London, The Silver Screen Archives, London Daily Mirror, Paris Match, Annan Photo Features, NBC, HBO, ABC Photographs, Reuters, Getty Images, Foto-Ad Inc, M.G.M, United Press Limited, Cine-Arte, Mirror pic, Associated Press, Wide World Photo's, Cinelandia, 20th Century Fox, Universal Pictures, Paramount Pictures, Pictorial Parade, Daily News, Authenticated Inc, Propiedad Tito Franco, B & H Productions, House Of Taylor, Elizabeth Arden Inc, Christies Auction House, Vivid Images Inc, Chen Sam & Associates, Movie Heaven, Long Photographs, Ron Galella Limited, La Scalia Autographs.

American Foundation for AIDS research, Elizabeth Aids foundation, Madam Alexander's, Franklin Mint, Turner Entertainment, Time Life Inc, Examiner Magazine, National Enquirer, The Earliest Bird, Google Earth, Andy Warhol, Harmonie Autographs and Music International, La Scala Autographs Inc, Foto.com, APF Annan Photo Features.

Keystone/Getty Images, Big Pictures, Barcroft Media, Australasian Picture Library, Austral, Perfumes International, Wire Images, PA/ Reuters, Blitz Pictures, Nikos, Image Bank, The Photo Library, Picture Media, Alpha Globe Photos, Snap /Rev Features, London Entertainment/ Splash News, Snapper Media, FotoPics, Classic Graphics and Changing Posters.

Lightning Source UK Ltd.
Milton Keynes UK
UKHW050814240619
344934UK00005B/11/P